DATE DUE

GAYLORD			PRINTED IN U.S.A.

Asherah and the Cult of Yahweh in Israel

THE SOCIETY OF BIBLICAL LITERATURE
MONOGRAPH SERIES

Adela Yarbro Collins, Editor
P. Kyle McCarter, Jr., Associate Editor

Number 34
ASHERAH AND THE CULT OF YAHWEH IN ISRAEL

by
Saul M. Olyan

Saul M. Olyan

ASHERAH AND THE CULT OF YAHWEH IN ISRAEL

Scholars Press
Atlanta, Georgia

ASHERAH AND THE CULT OF YAHWEH IN ISRAEL

by
Saul M. Olyan

Library of Congress Cataloging in Publication Data

Olyan, Saul.
    Asherah and the cult of Yahweh in Israel / Saul Olyan.
        p.   cm. -- (Monograph series / Society of Biblical Literature
 ; no. 34)
    Bibliography: p.
    ISBN 1-555-40253-4 (alk. paper). ISBN 1-555-40254-2)pbk. : alk.
paper)
    1. Asherah (Semitic deity)--Biblical teaching. 2. God--Worship
and love--Biblical teaching. 3. Bible. O.T.--Criticism,
interpretation, etc. I. Title. II. Series: Monograph series
(Society of Biblical Literature) ; no. 34.
BS1199.A77045   1988
221.9'5--dc19   88-19168

Printed in the United States of America
on acid-free paper

CONTENTS

ACKNOWLEDGMENTS

It is a pleasure for me to recognize my debt to teachers, colleagues, and students who have contributed to the development of this monograph over the past five years. A very early version of chapter two was delivered at the colloquium "New Trajectories in Biblical Studies" at York University in Toronto in November, 1982. In December, 1984, I had the opportunity to present a version of chapter one at the Society of Biblical Literature/American Schools of Oriental Research meetings in Chicago. The comments and criticisms I received at these sessions afforded me the opportunity to improve my argumentation.

A number of individuals have contributed to the genesis of this monograph. Frank Moore Cross, Paul D. Hanson, John Strugnell, Baruch Halpern and Larry Hurtado read the manuscript and offered suggestions toward its improvement. Dennis Pardee and Frank Moore Cross were kind enough to allow me to read and cite unpublished materials. I should like particularly to thank Mark S. Smith, Gary A. Anderson and Ronald S. Hendel, who were generous in their encouragement and rigorous in their criticism. My understanding of myths and symbols has been enriched by long hours of discussion with Gary Granzberg, head of Anthropology at the University of Winnipeg. Duncan Lennox, my research assistant, read the manuscript for errors and helped to prepare the index of authors cited. The University of Winnipeg provided a grant to pay his salary. Finally, I should like to thank P. Kyle McCarter, Jr., for his helpful suggestions during the final editorial stages. To these friends I offer my sincere thanks, and dedicate this volume to my parents Eve and Sidney Olyan with love.

Saul M. Olyan
Winnipeg and New Haven
Summer 1987

ABBREVIATIONS

AB	Anchor Bible
AfO	*Archiv für Orientforschung*
AHw	W. von Soden, *Akkadisches Handwörterbuch*
AJBA	*Australian Journal of Biblical Archaeology*
AJSL	*American Journal of Semitic Languages and Literatures*
ANEP	J.B. Pritchard, (ed.), *The Ancient Near East in Pictures*
ANET	_____, *Ancient Near Eastern Texts Relating to the Old Testament*
AnOr	Analecta Orientalia
AOAT	Alter Orient und Altes Testament
AOS	American Oriental Series
ATD	Das Alte Testament Deutsch
BA	*Biblical Archaeologist*
Bab.	Babylonian
BASOR	*Bulletin of the American Schools of Oriental Research*
BETL	Bibliotheca ephemeridum theologicum lovaniensium
BH	Biblical Hebrew
Bib	*Biblica*
Bib Leb	*Bibel und Leben*
BibOr	Biblica et Orientalia
BJRL	*Bulletin of the John Rylands University Library of Manchester*
BKAT	Biblischer Kommentar: Altes Testament
BZAW	Beihefte zur Zeitschrift für die alttestamentliche Wissenschaft
CAT	Commentaire de l'Ancien Testament
CBQ	*Catholic Biblical Quarterly*
CBQMS	Catholic Biblical Quarterly Monograph Series
CIL	*Corpus Inscriptionum Latinarum*
CIS	*Corpus Inscriptionum Semiticarum*

CTA	A. Herdner, (ed.), *Corpus des tablettes en cunéiformes alphabétiques*
DN	divine name
Dtr	The Deuteronomistic History
Dtr$_2$	Second (exilic) edition of Dtr
DTT	*Dansk teologisk tidsskrift*
FRLANT	Forschungen zur Religion und Literatur des Alten und Neuen Testaments
GN	geographic name
HAT	Handbuch zum Alten Testament
HSM	Harvard Semitic Monographs
HTR	*Harvard Theological Review*
HUCA	*Hebrew Union College Annual*
IDB	G.A. Buttrick (ed.), *Interpreter's Dictionary of the Bible*
IDBSup	*Interpreter's Dictionary of the Bible, Supplement*
IEJ	*Israel Exploration Journal*
Int	*Interpretation*
JAOS	*Journal of the American Oriental Society*
JBL	*Journal of Biblical Literature*
JCS	*Journal of Cuneiform Studies*
JNES	*Journal of Near Eastern Studies*
JPOS	*Journal of the Palestine Oriental Society*
JTS	*Journal of Theological Studies*
KAI	H. Donner and W. Röllig, *Kanaanäische und aramäische Inschriften*
KAT	Kommentar zum Alten Testament
KB	L. Köhler and W. Baumgartner, *Lexicon in Veteris Testamenti libros*
LB	Late Bronze
LXX	The Septuagint
MB	Middle Bronze
MDOG	*Mitteilungen der deutschen Orient-Gesellschaft*
MT	Massoretic Text
OLP	Orientalia Lovaniensia Periodica
Or	*Orientalia* (Rome)
PE	Eusebius of Caesarea, *Praeparatio Evangelica*
*PH	Proto-Hebrew
PN	personal name
PRU	*Le Palais royal d'Ugarit*
*PS	Proto-Semitic
RB	*Revue biblique*
SBLDS	Society of Biblical Literature Dissertation Series

SBLTT	Society of Biblical Literature Texts and Translations
Sef	*Sefarad*
Sem	*Semitica*
Syr	the Syriac (Pešiṭta) version
TDOT	G.J. Botterweck and H. Ringgren (eds.), *Theological Dictionary of the Old Testament*
TZ	*Theologische Zeitschrift*
UF	*Ugarit-Forschungen*
Ug. V	J. Nougayrol et al. (eds.), *Ugaritica V*
UT	C. Gordon, *Ugaritic Textbook*
WMyth	H.W. Haussig (ed.), *Wörterbuch der Mythologie*
VT	*Vetus Testamentum*
VTSup	Vetus Testamentum, Supplements
ZAW	*Zeitschrift für die alttestamentliche Wissenschaft*
ZDPV	*Zeitschrift des deutschen Palästina Vereins*
ZKT	*Zeitschrift für katholische Theologie*

INTRODUCTION

There has been much discussion of late in scholarly circles concerning Asherah, her cult symbol ("the asherah"), and their relationship to the cult of Yahweh in Israel. Most of this discussion has stemmed from the recent discovery of a cache of valuable inscriptions from Kuntillet Ajrûd, and a tomb inscription from Khirbet el-Qôm. There has been much debate among scholars concerning the interpretation of 'šrth in these inscriptions. Some scholars have argued that 'šrth is to be understood as a common noun meaning holy place, as in Phoenician or Akkadian ("his/its sanctuary"). Others have argued that 'šrth is the name of the goddess Asherah with pronominal suffix attached ("his/its Asherah"). Finally, a number of scholars have asserted that 'šrth is the common noun asherah, the well-attested cult symbol of the aforesaid goddess, with pronominal suffix attached ("his/its asherah"). The majority of commentators now favor the last position. If either of the latter two explanations is correct, we have new and valuable extra-biblical evidence for Asherah's role in Yahweh's cultus.

The major purpose of this monograph is to undertake a thorough investigation of the evidence pertaining to Asherah and her cult symbol in Israelite religion of the monarchic era. There has been much discussion of this subject, but no attempt has yet been made to deal with the evidence thoroughly and comprehensively. Our study begins with an examination of all references and alleged references to Asherah or her cult symbol in the Hebrew Bible. A number of questions will be asked in the process: Which writers or editors oppose Asherah and her cult symbol? What role might Asherah or her symbol have played in Yahweh's cult? Which groups in Israel might have been devoted to Asherah's worship? Was her worship an element only of popular religion, as many scholars believe, or an aspect of the official cult, or both? What might have motivated opposition to Asherah and her symbol? The second chapter entails an examination of the relevant epigraphic and archeological data from Israel. The various interpretations of these data will be evaluated, and their implications for understanding Israelite religion discussed, particularly in light of the biblical evidence. The third and fourth chapters present an examination of the evidence from Canaanite religion as it pertains to Asherah. We shall consider whether the data of the second and first millennium BCE support the claims of certain biblical writers (specifically the deuteronomistic school) that Asherah is the consort of Baal in the first millennium BCE. Perhaps her association with Baal serves some polemical purpose.

The position that the goddess Asherah was Yahweh's consort has been argued by a number of scholars in recent years and appears to be gaining in credibility. Proponents have based their arguments for the most part on the evidence from Kuntillet Ajrûd. Since Asherah was El's main consort in Canaanite religion, her pairing with Yahweh, who is identified with El by biblical writers, would make sense.[1] In light of the intense rivalry between Baal and Yahweh and their respective votaries during the period of the divided monarchy, it would make little sense for the two gods to share the same consort.

---

[1] On the identification of El and Yahweh, see J. Wellhausen, *Prolegomena to the History of Israel* (repr. Gloucester, MA: Peter Smith, 1973) 433 n.1, and the detailed treatment of F.M. Cross, "Yahweh and the God of the Patriarchs," *HTR* 55 (1962) 225-59. The identification is explicit in P (Exod 6:6), and implied in J (Exod 3:16) and E (Exod 3:6, 15).

Chapter 1

ASHERAH IN THE HEBREW BIBLE

The role of Asherah and her cult symbol in Israelite religion has been much discussed of late.[1] Biblical and extrabiblical evidence seem to indicate that the asherah was not a living tree, but rather a stylized tree (probably a date palm) or perhaps a pole in some cases.[2] The use of verbs such as "make" (' $\acute{S}H$)[3]

[1] See most recently P. Kyle McCarter, Jr., "Aspects of the Religion of the Israelite Monarchy," in *Ancient Israelite Religion: Essays in Honor of Frank Moore Cross*, ed. P.D. Miller, et al. (Philadelphia: Fortress, 1987) 137-55; W.A. Maier, III, *'Ašerah: Extrabiblical Evidence* (HSM 37; Atlanta: Scholars, 1986); J. Tigay, *You Shall Have No Other Gods. Israelite Religion in the Light of Hebrew Inscriptions* (HSS 31; Atlanta: Scholars, 1986) 26-30; J. Day, "Asherah in the Hebrew Bible and Northwest Semitic Literature," *JBL* 105 (1986) 385-408; W. Dever, "Asherah, Consort of Yahweh? New Evidence from Kuntillet ' Ajrûd," *BASOR* 255 (1984) 21-37; A. Lemaire, "Date et origine des inscriptions hébraïques et phéniciennes de Kuntillet ' Ajrud," *Studi epigraphici e linguistici* 1 (1984) 131-43; M. Weinfeld, "Kuntillet ' Ajrud Inscriptions and their Significance," *Studi epigraphici e linguistici* 1 (1984) 121-30; A. Angerstorfer, "Asherah als 'consort of Jahwe' oder Ashirtah?" *Biblische Notizen* 17 (1982) 7-16; Dever, "Material Remains and the Cult in Ancient Israel: An Essay in Archaeological Systematics," in *The Word of the Lord Shall Go Forth: Essays in Honor of David Noel Freedman in Celebration of His Sixtieth Birthday*, ed. C. L. Meyers and M. O'Conner (Winona Lake, IN: Eisenbrauns, 1983) 571-87; "Recent Archaeological Confirmation of the Cult of Asherah in Ancient Israel," *Hebrew Studies* 23 (1982) 37-44; J. Emerton, "New Light on Israelite Religion: The Implications of the Inscriptions from Kuntillet ' Ajrud," *ZAW* 94 (1982) 2-20; M. Gilula, "To Yahweh Shomron and to his Asherah," *Shnaton* 3 (1978/79) 129-37 (Hebrew); A. Lemaire, "Les inscriptions de Khirbet el-Qôm et l'Ashérah de Yhwh," *RB* 84 (1977) 597-608; E. Lipiński, "The Goddess Aṭirat in Ancient Arabia, in Babylonia, and in Ugarit," *OLP* 3 (1972) 101-19, especially 116, where he argues "that no biblical passage mentions the goddess Aṭirat or her emblem." J.C. de Moor, "'*ăshērāh*," in *Theological Dictionary of the Old Testament*, ed. G.J. Botterweck and H. Ringgren, tr. J.T. Willis (Grand Rapids: Eerdmans, 1974) 1:438-44; M. Pope, "Aṭirat," in Pope and W. Röllig, "Syrien. Die Mythologie der Ugariter und Phönizier," *WMyth* 1:246-49.

[2] For discussion, see Lemaire, "Les inscriptions," 606-607, de Moor, "'*ashērāh*," 441-43, and Pope, "Atirat" 246. Pope points out the probable relationship of Asherah and the date palm based on South Arabic sources: "Eine Deutung stellt ihn zusammen mit *'atir* 'Freund,' einem Epithet der arab. Palmbaumgöttin. Diese Verbindung mit einem Baum könnte die spätere Identifikation der A. mit einem Baum oder Pfahl. . .erklären." At Kuntillet Ajrûd, on pithos A, a drawing appears of a stylized tree poised over the back of a lion. Ibexes appear on either side of the

"build" (*BNH*)[4] or "erect" (*NṢB*, *ʿMD* [Hipʿil])[5] indicate this.[6] In a few cases, it seems as if the asherah were a wooden likeness of the goddess: *wayyāśem ʾet-pesel hāʾăšērâ ʾăšer ʿāśâ babbayit*, "He placed the graven image of the asherah which he had made in the house. . ." (2 Kgs 21:7).[7] LXX translates Hebrew *ʾăšērâ* regularly with *alsos*, plural *alsē*, "grove(s)," except in Isa 17:8

tree. P. Beck ("The Drawings from Horvat Teiman [Kuntillet ʿAjrûd]," *Tel Aviv* 9 [1982] 3-86, especially 13-16) points out that the tree shares traits with comparable Phoenician examples (lotus and bud, capital with volutes). She does not comment on the relationship of the tree, lion and ibexes, though she points out that the same combination of figures appears on the Tel Taanak cult stand of the tenth century (see P. Lapp, "The 1968 Excavations at Tell Taʿannek," *BASOR* 195 [1969] 2-49, and "A Ritual Incense Stand from Taanak," *Qadmoniot* 2 [1969] 16-17). Near Ras Shamra (Minet el-Beida), an ivory in Mycenean style was discovered which portrays a goddess flanked by two animals eating plants from her hands (*Ugaritica 1* frontispiece and *ANEP* 464). J. Gray (*The Canaanites* [London: Thames and Hudson, 1964] 231 n.32) has argued that there is a significant relationship between this scene and the common Phoenician motif of the palm tree flanked by two ibexes. On the relationship of the lion to the goddess Asherah, see the discussion of F. M. Cross, *Canaanite Myth and Hebrew Epic* (Cambridge: Harvard University, 1973) 33-35. Qudšu (=Asherah) is sometimes portrayed standing on the back of a lion in Egyptian stelae (*ANEP* 471, 473, 474, where the goddess is identified as Qudšu, and 470, 472 where she is not identified). It is thus no surprise that the palm tree of Ajrûd pithos A is poised over the back of a lion, a natural throne for Asherah or her symbol. On tree symbolism and Asherah, see also R. Oden, *Studies in Lucian's De Syria Dea* (HSM 15; Missoula, MT: Scholars, 1977) 142-55. Oden discusses the Punic caduceus, arguing that it is a stylized palm. He also explores insightfully the relationship of the caduceus/palm and other Tannit symbols to the Hierapolis *sēmēion*. See also the recent discussion of Maier, *ʾAšerah*.

[3] 1 Kgs 14:15; 16:33; 2 Kgs 17:16; 21:3; Isa 17:8; 2 Chr 33:3.

[4] 1 Kgs 14:23. An odd usage, though in a list of things one can normally "build."

[5] 2 Kgs 17:10; 2 Chr 33:19. For verbs used of the asherah, see W.L. Reed, *The Asherah in the Old Testament* (Fort Worth: Texas Christian University, 1949) 29-37.

[6] Deut 16:21 complicates matters by using the verb "to plant" (*NṬʿ*): *lōʾ- tiṭṭaʿ lĕkā ʾăšērâ kol-ʿēṣ ʾēṣel mizbaḥ Yahweh ʾĕlōhêkā ʾăšer taʿăśeh-lāk*. It is not a living tree because the law seems to distinguish it from real trees (*ʿēṣ*), yet oddly, the verb "to plant" is used. The evidence on the whole is ambiguous, and so it is impossible in every case to determine the precise nature of an asherah. See Pope, "Atirat," 246. De Moor ("*ʾăšērāh*," 442) cites evidence that *NṬʿ* can be used in a non-literal sense if one intends to drive a pole into the ground (Qoh 12:11).

[7] Also 1 Kgs 15:12-13, where Asa destroys a *mipleṣet lāʾăšērâ*, "an abominable image of/for Asherah" (or "the asherah"). The noun is derived from the rare verbal root *PLṢ*, "to shudder," which occurs once in the Hitpaʿel (Job 9:6, *yitpallāṣûn*). A noun *pallāṣût*, "shuddering," is also attested (Job 21:6; Isa 21:4; Ezek 7:18; Ps 55:6). Thus, one can say that a *mipleṣet* appears to be an image which causes horror or shuddering. As a number of scholars have pointed out, the distinction between a god and his/her symbol is vague at best; often this is indicated by the sharing of the same name, as in the case of Asherah/the asherah (see de Moor, ibid. 441-42). See 2 Kgs 21:3, 7; 23:4, 6 for Asherah and her symbol mentioned in the same passages. The use of the article before the goddess's name in 1 Kgs 15:13 and 2 Kgs 21:7 is

and 27:9, where *dendra*, "tree," is utilized, and 2 Chr 15:16 and 24:18, where confusion results in "Astarte." Jerome, following LXX, translates *lucus* or *nemus*. It is possible that LXX *alsos* referred to a sacred area or object, and not just a grove. In Classical Greek the word came to refer to a sacred precinct, even one without trees. In fact *alsos* corresponds to *bāmôt* in Mic 3:12 (=Jer 26:18). In general, the Targum retains the Hebrew word *'ăšērâ* where it occurs in the Hebrew Bible. The Pešiṭṭa takes the object as an image of some kind, employing various words.[8] Thus, the versions are of little help in determining the exact nature of the biblical asherah. Rather than attempt to determine exactly what the asherah was, we intend in this chapter to investigate in some detail the relationship of the asherah to the cult of Yahweh, based on the biblical evidence. We shall assume that the asherah was a stylized tree, probably a representation of the date palm.

Where do we find anti-asherah polemic in the Hebrew Bible? We argue that such polemic is restricted to the Deuteronomistic History or to materials which betray the influence of deuteronomistic language and theology.[9] The lack of concern for the asherah (or Asherah) as reflected in the literary remains of other Israelite circles opposed to the worship of Baal suggests that among these groups the cult symbol was not considered illegitimate or non-Yahwistic. This is intriguing. It is extremely difficult to explain why one group of anti-Baal Yahwists (Dtr) would oppose the asherah while other anti-Baal circles seem not to have opposed it, and possibly even approved of it. The deuteronomistic concern for the asherah is often found together with opposition to the altars and sanctuaries outside of Jerusalem, yet this observation is no solution to the problem, for any asherah of the Jerusalem temple is also condemned.[10] Do we find in the anti-asherah theology of the deuteronomists the be-

---

not unusual. Often *habba'al* appears where we would expect simply *ba'al* (1 Kgs 16:32).

[8] See the discussion of Reed (*The Asherah* 6-10) and, recently, Day ("Asherah," 397-98, 401-404) on the history of interpretation particularly.

[9] For example, Chronicles passages taken from the *Vorlage* of the Deuteronomistic History or passages in prophetic books or the Pentateuch which display the telltale signs of deuteronomistic editing. See the discussion ahead on Exod 34:13; Isa 17:8; 27:9; Jer 17:2; Mic 5:13. A. Lemaire observed briefly the polemical nature of the treatment of the asherah in the Deuteronomistic History in "Les inscriptions," 605-606.

[10] 1 Kgs 14:23; 2 Kgs 13:6; 17:9-12; 18:4; 21:3 with altars and sanctuaries outside Jerusalem. See 1 Kgs 15:13(?); 2 Kgs 18:4-5(?); 21:7; 23:6 for the condemnation of asherahs in the Jerusalem temple.

ginnings of a thoroughgoing monotheism? This seems unlikely
in view of statements in Deut 4:19 and 29:25, which build on the
poetry of 32:8-9, where the other nations are the inheritance of
the other gods.[11] There is no sense in these passages that the
other gods do not exist; only that Israel cannot worship them.
Similarly, deuteronomistic opposition to Asherah and her symbol might be the result of logical extension of Yahweh's exclusive claim on Israel as his *naḥălâ*. As far as other anti-Baal
groups are concerned, we know of no positive statements about
the asherah as a legitimate cult symbol, yet the silence is telling,
as is the fact that Jehu left the asherah of Samaria standing after
his coup and anti-Baal reform.

The deuteronomistic polemic against the asherah or Asherah
is usually found in highly rhetorical speeches concerning the
sins of Israel and/or Judah against Yahweh. The peroration
against Samaria in 2 Kgs 17:16-17 best illustrates this pattern.
The asherah, along with the high places, the bull icons of the
northern cult, the host of heaven, Baal, human sacrifice, divination and sorcery, is condemned as a non-Yahwistic practice in-
herited from the surrounding nations: "And they forsook all the
commandments of Yahweh their God, and made for themselves
molten images of two calves; and they made an asherah, and
prostrated themselves to all the host of heaven, and served Baal.
They burned their sons and daughters [as an offering], and made
use of divination and sorcery, and sold themselves to do evil in
the eyes of Yahweh, provoking him to anger." This kind of association and condemnation is typical of deuteronomistic polemic,
as other passages illustrate.[12] In some passages, the asherah is
associated specifically with the Jerusalem temple or other
Yahwistic shrines in Judah (2 Kgs 18:4; 21:7; 23:6, 14), or the reform cult of Jeroboam in the north (1 Kgs 14:15-16; 2 Kgs
23:15).[13]

Is the asherah "Canaanite," as the deuteronomistic polemic
would have it? Do these texts describe "syncretism" in the cult?
Many scholars speak of "syncretism" or "pagan influences" in
the Israelite cult when they speak about the asherah, as if it re-

[11] See the discussion ahead on these passages. On incipient monotheism, see
F. Stolz, "Monotheismus in Israel," in *Monotheismus im alten Israel und seiner
Umwelt*, ed. O. Keel (Biblische Beiträge 14; Fribourg: Schweizerisches Kath-
olisches Bibelwerk, 1980) 143-89.

[12] Deut 7:2-8; 12:2-3; 1 Kgs 14:23; 2 Kgs 18:4, 12. See the discussion ahead on the
treatment of Jeroboam's reform cult in the Deuteronomistic History, and Cross,
Canaanite Myth 73-75, 198-200.

[13] In 2 Kgs 18:4, the asherah is associated with the bronze serpent, the ancient
Yahwistic cult symbol perhaps related to Asherah. See our treatment ahead.

ally were a non-Yahwistic borrowing from the "Canaanites."[14]
These terms suggest that the asherah was originally foreign to
the cult of Yahweh, but this view is not supported even by the
biblical evidence. W.L. Reed raises a relevant question about
the asherah and the Yahwistic cult: Why in the patriarchal narratives is it permissible for trees to be planted in Yahwistic cult
places (e.g. Gen 21:33)? Reed argues that this indicates the
asherah must have been a graven image of the goddess and not
a tree, or it would not have been condemned. This attempt at
harmonization is no solution. The crux of the problem is the
conflict between the deuteronomistic anti-asherah theology and
the patriarchal traditions about trees at cult places, not the question of whether the asherah was a tree (either living or stylized)
or an image. Whether tree or image, the asherah would represent the goddess in the cult. The patriarchal narratives of cult
founding at Bethel, Hebron and Beersheba indicate that the sacred tree and the pillar (*maṣṣēbâ*) were legitimate in the
Yahwistic cult early on, and were not considered illegitimate in
the time of the Yahwist or the Elohist.[15] Even in texts of the
Deuteronomistic History relating the events of the monarchic

[14] This tendency reflects a willingness to believe the polemical statements of the
deuteronomists about the asherah: Deut 7:1-5; 12:1-3; 2 Kgs 17:9 ff. See the remarks of Day, "Asherah," 392, 399-400, 406: "A Canaanite accretion to the cult of
the God of Sinai"; Tigay, *No Other Gods* 26 (the cult with the asherah is "hetero-
dox" and "may point in the direction of paganism"); Z. Meshel, "Did Yahweh Have
A Consort?" *Biblical Archaeology Review* 5.2 (1979) 28; Reed, *The Asherah* 39, 41;
R. Patai, "The Goddess Asherah," *JNES* 24 (1965) 45-48 (Asherah's cult is "pagan
worship"); de Moor, "'ăshērāh," 444; Emerton, "New Light," 14 ("there is no difficulty in supposing that Asherah may have been the wife of Yahweh in such a *syncretistic* cult. . . ." [my emphasis]).

[15] Reed, *The Asherah* 42. See Gen 12:8 (J), where Abraham builds an altar at
Bethel; Gen 21:33 (J), a Beersheba cult etiology, where Abraham plants an *'ēšel*
(tamarisk) and calls on the name of Yahweh *'ēl 'ôlām*, thereby founding the cult at
Beersheba; Gen 26:23-25 (J), a parallel account of the founding of Beersheba's cult,
this time by Isaac, who sets up an altar there. This is an oral variant of Gen 33:20;
Gen 28:11-22 (JE), the Bethel cult legend, where a *maṣṣēbâ* is erected to mark the
place of the *bêt 'ēl* by Jacob. The *maṣṣēbâ*, like the asherah, is condemned by the
deuteronomistic school as a "Canaanite" fertility symbol, often specifically as a
symbol of Baal (Deut 7:5; 12:3; 16:22; 2 Kgs 17:10, etc.). There is evidence that the
maṣṣēbâ was a legitimate Yahwistic symbol in at least some non-deuteronomistic
circles. Besides Genesis 28, see Gen 31:13, 45; 35:14, 20; and Exod 24:4, where
Moses builds an altar with twelve pillars at the foot of the holy mountain. The
maṣṣēbâ is also forbidden in P legal material (Exod 23:24; Lev 26:1), however the
asherah is not. Pillars were found in the holy of holies of the Arad temple. See C.
Graesser, Jr., "Standing Stones in Ancient Palestine," *BA* 35 (1972) 34-63; E. Stockton, "Stones at Worship," *AJBA* 1 (1970) 58-81. The prophetic critique of the *maṣṣēbâ* in the book of Hosea does not associate it with the cult of Baal, but with
Yahwistic practice (Hos 3:4, with the ephod and teraphim, and 10:1, 2, with altars).

period, we find evidence that the asherah was associated not with Baal but with the cult of Yahweh.

We shall begin with the asherah of Samaria, which Ahab erected (1 Kgs 16:32-33): *wayyāqem mizbēaḥ labbā'al bêt habba'al 'ăšer bānâ běšōměrôn wayya'aś 'aḥāb 'et-hā'ăšērâ*, "And he [Ahab] erected an altar for Baal in the temple of Baal which he built in Samaria. And Ahab made the asherah. . . ." There are scholars who have cited this text as evidence of Asherah's alleged association with Baal in Iron Age Israel. Some have claimed that Jezebel imported the worship of Asherah along with that of Baal from her native Phoenicia.[16] But a careful reading of the Hebrew does not indicate association. There is no ambiguity in the syntax. A new sentence describes the asherah. Ahab did not place it "there" (*šām*), that is, in the temple of Baal. We do not know from this text where it was located. Other passages shed light on the problem, indicating that it did not stand in the Baal shrine. In the narratives of Jehu's coup and subsequent anti-Baal reform (2 Kings 9-10),[17] there is no men-

---

[16] The majority of scholars have assumed that Asherah is the consort of Baal in the Iron Age. See W.F. Albright, *Archaeology and the Religion of Israel* (Baltimore: Johns Hopkins University, 1942) 73, 76. Cross, *Canaanite Myth* 32: "Later, especially in biblical notices, she is the consort of Ba'l." R. de Vaux, *Ancient Israel* (New York: McGraw-Hill, 1961) 285-86: "Achab installed an *'asherah* according to 1 K 16:33 and a *maṣṣebah* according to 2 K 3:2, in the temple of Baal at Samaria. . . . The Ras Shamra texts mention the goddess Asherah as the consort of the god El, and in the Bible she is the consort of Baal." G. Ahlström (*Aspects of Syncretism in Israelite Religion* [Lund: Gleerup, 1963] 51 n.4) believes Ahab made the asherah for Baal's temple. Pope, "Atirat," 249: "Im AT ist der Vorgang abgeschlossen und A. erscheint immer neben B̄aal, während El keine Rolle mehr spielt." See also de Moor, "'ăšērāh," 411. Patai, "The Goddess Asherah," 40, 47. Dever ("Asherah," 29) thinks that Asherah and Aštart are "interchangeable consorts of Ba'al in the Hebrew Bible." We do not agree. See the detailed discussion ahead in Chapter 3 on the associations of Asherah in Canaanite religion. H. Wilderberger, *Jesaja 13-27* (BKAT 10/7-12; Neukirchen-Vluyn: Neukirchener, 1974-78) 653-55: "Im Alten Testament gehört Aschera mit Baal zusammen. . . ." U. Oldenburg, *The Conflict Between El and Ba'al in Canaanite Religion* (Leiden: Brill, 1969) 145; K.-H. Bernhardt, "Aschera in Ugarit und im Alten Testament," *Mitteilungen des Instituts für Orientforschung* 13 (1967) 163-74; recently J.W. Betlyon, "The Cult of 'Asherah/'Ēlat at Sidon," *JNES* 44 (1985) 55; G. Mendenhall, "The Worship of Baal and Asherah: A Study in the Social Bonding Function of Religious Systems," in *Biblical and Related Studies Presented to Samuel Iwry*, ed. A. Kort and S. Morschauser (Winona Lake, IN: Eisenbrauns, 1985) 157; Day, "Asherah," 399; Maier, *'Ašerah* 100.

[17] Embedded within the Deuteronomistic History are two separate narratives concerning Jehu. 2 Kings 9 is a propaganda piece of high literary style intended to justify Jehu's coup as the execution of Yahweh's will for Israel and against Omri's house. It probably stems from the age of Jeroboam II (ca. 783-48), when the dynasty of Jehu had come under attack in some circles for the violence of its founder's

tion of the asherah of Samaria.[18] Jehu, an ultraconservative supported both by the Elijah-Elisha school and the Rechabites, destroys the Baal temple and the devotees of Baal after an elaborate ruse. Yet we are told that his reform did not include the Bethel-Dan cult established by Jeroboam, nor did it remove the asherah of Samaria, which remained standing long after his death (2 Kgs 13:6). If the asherah, like the Bethel-Dan cult, had been thought illegitimate by these conservative Yahwists, some measure of reform should have taken place. But it did not. Certainly if the asherah had been a part of the cult of Baal, it would have perished in Jehu's reform. Thus, there is evidence within the Deuteronomistic History itself that the asherah really was not associated with the cult of Baal.[19] But with whose cult was it associated? Cumulative evidence suggests strongly the cult of Yahweh. An asherah stood in the Bethel temple (2 Kgs 23:15), and other asherahs were set up at various high places. We shall argue that the asherah of Samaria must have stood in a sanctuary dedicated to Yahweh *šōměrôn*.

An investigation of northern prophecy reveals a similar lack of opposition to the asherah, which indirectly suggests approval and legitimacy. Hosea, who opposes Baal strenuously, and even criticizes the bull icons of Bethel, never mentions the asherah.[20]

coup (see Hos 1:4-5). On Jehu's close connections with the conservative Elijah-Elisha school, see Olyan, "*Hāšālôm*: Some Literary Considerations of 2 Kings 9," *CBQ* 46 (1984) 652-68. 2 Kings 10, set off from the preceding narrative by a disjunction and lacking the same literary motifs, describes Jehu's elimination of the remaining Omrides in Samaria and his destruction of Baal's temple there.

[18] This has been noticed by other scholars. Ahlström (*Aspects of Syncretism* 50-53) notes that Jehu allowed the asherah to remain standing. He argues correctly that the asherah was not a foreign import from Phoenicia but a part of the native Israelite cult, though he assumes erroneously that the asherah of Samaria stood in Baal's temple (51 n.4). See also Patai, "The Goddess Asherah," 46, and S. Timm, *Die Dynastie Omri* (FRLANT 124; Göttingen: Vandenhoeck & Ruprecht, 1982) 39-40, 297-300, and n.42. Timm states that "die Ašera in Samaria muß den Sturm der Revolution Jehus schadlos überstanden haben." He points out that it could not have stood in the Baal temple, and believes that the asherah possessed a particular popular appeal, but he does not draw out the implications of his observations. The asherah must have been a legitimate cult symbol in the eyes of Jehu and his conservative supporters or it would have been destroyed. Timm, like Ahlström, argues that the cult of Asherah was not a foreign import into Israel by way of Jezebel, yet he erroneously accepts the text of 1 Kgs 18:19, which mentions four hundred prophets of Asherah in an obvious editorial gloss on the story, where they play no role whatsoever. See our discussion of this passage ahead.

[19] On the "sin of Jeroboam," see 1 Kgs 12:30; 13:1-2, where Josiah is even mentioned by name; 2 Kgs 17:21-23; 23:15. Jeroboam's real crime was the creation of a cult to rival Jerusalem.

[20] The bulls are mentioned in Hos 8:5-6; 10:5-6 and 13:2. Baal is mentioned in 9:10;

Amos never discusses the asherah, Baal or the bull icons. Some scholars have cited 1 Kgs 18:19 as evidence both for the association of Baal and Asherah in the Iron Age and for the opposition of Elijah to Asherah.[21] The verse mentions 400 prophets of Asherah, along with 450 prophets of Baal who ate at Jezebel's table. Yet the mention of the prophets of Asherah is a textual gloss, notwithstanding the arguments of some scholars to the contrary.[22] Although the prophets of Baal play a central role in the narrative as Elijah's foils and the representatives of Yahweh's archrival, the prophets of Asherah play no role. In fact, they are not mentioned again.[23] In contrast, the prophets of Baal are mentioned four times in the text, and Baal himself five times. As some scholars have noted, the Hexapla marks the prophets of Asherah with an asterisk, indicating that they are an addition to the text of LXX.[24] All of these observations lead to the conclusion that there were no prophets of Asherah in the original text. Their presence can be explained with the suggestion that an editor, schooled in deuteronomistic anti-asherah ideology, added what he perceived to be a natural expansion of the text. In light of the fact that the text was subject to deuteronomistic redaction, this is not an unlikely hypothesis.

11:2; and 13:1. If the asherah were a part of Baal's cult, we should expect it to be condemned here, but it is not even mentioned.

[21] De Moor, "'ăshērāh," 441; Reed, The Asherah 55, and "Asherah," IDB 1:251.

[22] Pope, "Atirat," 246: "Die Erwähnung der 400 Propheten der A. neben 450 Baalspropheten (1. Reg. 18, 19) wurde als Glosse betrachtet, doch ohne Grund, da ja auch der Taanak-Brief einen Wahrsager der Götten erwähnt." This argument is not convincing. Even if we accept Albright's reading u-ma-an ᵈA-ši-rat (assuming defective *umân for *ummân), this proves nothing with regard to the biblical text in question. There is now in fact doubt about the Taanak reading altogether. See A.F. Rainey, "Verbal Usages in the Tannach Texts," Israel Oriental Studies 7 (1977) 59, cited by Maier, 'Ašerah 179 n.26. Even if we were to accept the emendation, it would suggest only that Asherah had a religious specialist of some sort (?) in the Late Bronze Age. See Albright, "A Prince of Taanach in the Fifteenth Century B.C.," BASOR 94 (1944) 12-27, especially 18. He translates *ummân as "wizard." Many other scholars have recognized the gloss in 1 Kgs 18:19. Recently, see Emerton, "New Light," 16; Lipiński, "The Goddess Atirat," 114; Day, "Asherah," 400-401. Timm (Dynastie Omri 73 and n.82) argues that it should not be considered a gloss.

[23] LXX mentions the prophets of Asherah again in v 22, where it repeats the information in v 19, but this should be considered an expansion on v 19, to give a sense of symmetry to the passage where none exists in the MT (the Asherah prophets are not mentioned again in the actual narrative). Thus, against Reed (The Asherah 55), who believes it is as likely that MT lost *nĕbî'ê hā'ăšērâ through haplography as it is that the LXX phrase was added as a second gloss, but he provides no satisfactory explanation for this on text-critical grounds.

[24] Emerton, "New Light," 16 and Lipiński, "The Goddess Atirat," 114 have pointed this out, as well as Day, "Asherah," 400-401.

The evidence from Judah provides us with a less complex picture. Aside from the time of cultic reforms under Asa, Hezekiah and Josiah, the asherah seems to have played a role in the cult of Yahweh, in the Jerusalem temple and at various other sanctuaries, as it did in the north. In 1 Kgs 15:12-13, Asa is said to have removed Maacah from being queen mother, because she made an "abominable image" for Asherah (*mipleṣet lā'ăšērâ*).[25] He cut it down and burned it. In 2 Kgs 18:4 Hezekiah removes an asherah, presumably from the Jerusalem temple. Soon after this, Manasseh makes a new one and places it in the temple (2 Kgs 21:3, 7). Josiah destroys it (2 Kgs 23:4, 6, 7) as well as the asherahs of the high places (23:14) and that of the Bethel sanctuary (23:15), which had continued to operate after the fall of the north. In Judah we witness a struggle for royal support between the proponents of the deuteronomistic ideology and those who defend traditional worship. The deuteronomistic school are evidently the innovators, though in their polemic they claim that their position is traditional and ancient.[26]

The biblical evidence from both the north and the south suggests that the asherah was a standard and legitimate part of the cult of Yahweh in non-deuteronomistic circles, probably even among very conservative groups, as the Jehu traditions and the silence of the books of Amos and Hosea seem to indicate. The law in Deut 16:21 is also indicative of this: *lō' tiṭṭa'lĕkā 'ăšērâ kol-'ēṣ 'ēṣel mizbaḥ Yahweh 'ĕlōhêkā 'ăšer ta'ăśeh-lāk*, "You shall not plant for yourself an asherah—any tree—beside the altar of Yahweh your God which you make for yourself." There would be no need for such a prohibition if this were not a common practice. What, then, of deuteronomistic passages where Asherah or her symbol are associated with Baal? In Judg 6:25, 28, and 30, an asherah stands by Baal's altar, and in Judg 3:7 we are told that "the people of Israel did what was evil in the eyes of Yahweh, forgetting Yahweh their God and serving the Baals and the Asherahs." At the same time, a number of passages in the Deuteronomistic History associate Baal with Aštart (Biblical

---

[25] See note 8.

[26] G.W. Ahlström has made some important observations about the religion of Israel in the monarchic era. He argues that the asherah, like the high places and *maṣṣēbôt*, was a legitimate part of the cult of Yahweh. The reformers Hezekiah and Josiah should be seen as the radicals, and Manasseh as the traditionalist. He notes that many scholars are too quick to accept the narrator's views on Manasseh. They are polemical (*Royal Administration and National Religion in Ancient Palestine* [Leiden: Brill, 1982] 68-80).

Hebrew *'aštōret*, plural *'aštārōt*): Judg 2:13; 10:6; 1 Sam 7:3, 4; 12:10; 1 Kgs 11:5, 33; 2 Kgs 23:13, where she is called *šiqqûṣ ṣîdōnîm*. This association of Baal with Aštart is precisely what we should expect in the Iron Age, where Aštart is Baal's major consort in Canaanite religion.[27] There seems to be a confusion of the terms *'ăšērâ* and *'aštōret/'aštārôt* in the Deuteronomistic History.[28] Is this a willful confusion, or does it reflect a lack of distinction between the goddesses in this period?[29] Since for the

---

[27] See our discussion ahead. The Sidon cult is accurately reflected here. Aštart was the primary deity there.

[28] Compare for example Judg 3:7, *wayya'ăśû bĕnê-yiśrā'ēl 'et- hāra' bĕ'ênê Yahweh wayyiškĕhû 'et-Yahweh 'ĕlōhêhem wayya'abĕdû 'et-habbĕ'ālîm wĕ'et-hā'ăšērôt*, to Judg 2:13, *wayya'azĕbû 'et-Yahweh wayya'abĕdû labba'al wĕlā'aštārôt*. The distinct language and style of the deuteronomistic school is present in both passages, yet in the first, it is Asherah who is associated with Baal, but in the second, it is Aštart. It is as if the two are interchangeable in the theology of the deuteronomistic school. The form of Aštart's name in the Hebrew Bible, *'aštōret*, plural *'aštārôt*, deserves comment. The correct vocalization * *'aštart-* is secure from extra-biblical sources (Ugarit, late first millennium transcriptions), so how can one explain the unexpected shift *$*a > ō$* in the biblical form of the name? Some scholars suggest a polemical vocalization in the Bible meant to reflect *bōšet*, "shame," (thus *'aštōret*). See Pope, "Aštart," 250. If this explanation is not accepted, one must posit an unusual linguistic shift in Hebrew (from *$*a > ō$*) in its stead.

[29] Some scholars have argued that whatever distinctions existed between the three major Canaanite goddesses early on have broken down by the time of the deuteronomistic writers, and thus the divine names Asherah and Aštart are used synonymously. See de Moor, "'ăšērāh," 441. R. Oden (*De Syria Dea* 94-98, and "The Persistence of Canaanite Religion," *BA* 39 [1976] 31-36) argues that in Canaanite religion, the three major goddesses Asherah, Anat and Aštart could be associated with El or Baal. We do not agree with this hypothesis, and this will become clear in our discussion. Dever ("Asherah," 28-29) argues that there is evidence for the fusion of the major goddesses after the Late Bronze Age. There is indeed evidence that deities fused in Canaanite religion, forming new hypostases (Tannit 'aštart of the Sarepta Plaque, see ahead), but aside from the production of fusion deities the goddesses remained distinct down to the end of the first millennium. The examples of fusion demonstrate the mechanism in Canaanite religion for the production of new divinities through the combination of two established gods, one aspect of hypostatization. The "combination" deity produced by this fusion has independent existence from both of the two deities whose names it carries. Thus, for example, Tannit 'aštart, Aštart and Tannit are three separate deities in the Phoenician pantheon. Mulk 'aštart is considered a god and not a goddess—he does not replace or represent Aštart in the pantheon. Anatyahû is mentioned in the same sentence as Yahweh at Elephantine, but it is a separate deity. See our discussion ahead with citations and additional bibliography. Reed (*The Asherah* 54) explains the apparent confusion of Asherah and Aštart in the deuteronomistic passages differently. He suggests not that the two goddesses were fused by this time, but that the deuteronomistic writers had no interest in the details of Canaanite religion: "As far as he [the Deuteronomist] was concerned there may have been very little difference between them." Yet Reed does not argue for willful confusion. Lemaire, insightfully,

most part the goddesses remain distinct in Canaanite religion down to the late first millennium,[30] and since the deuteronomistic writers can be shown to employ purposeful distortion in polemic against rival cults, the former is the more appealing explanation.

Willful confusion certainly explains the deuteronomistic polemic against the reform cult of Jeroboam in the north. Jeroboam is presented as the founder of a new cult devoted to bull-gods in place of Yahweh: *kēn ʿāśâ běbêt ʾēl lězabbēaḥ lā ʿăgālîm ʾăšer ʿāśâ . . .*, "Thus he did in Bethel, sacrificing to the calves which he had made. . ." (1 Kgs 12:32). The deuteronomists even have Jeroboam credit the bulls with the saving acts of Yahweh in Egypt: "Behold your gods, O Israel, who brought you up out of the land of Egypt" (1 Kgs 12:28). The deuteronomistic writers also claim that Jeroboam presided over the investiture of a non-Levitic priesthood for his new royal sanctuaries (1 Kgs 12:25-33). All this is hardly possible in light of Jeroboam's weak position as a new king with a nascent kingdom to secure. The last thing such a king would do is innovate in the cult, and the invention of a new religion is inconceivable. Jeroboam's real "crime" was his establishment of two rival sanctuaries dedicated to Yahweh in order to draw northern pilgrims away from Jerusalem so that he could secure the independence of the north (see 1 Kgs 12:27-28).[31]

A second example of such willful confusion involves the cult of human sacrifice in Israel. In deuteronomistic materials, we find a polemic against an alleged god Molek, to whom human sacrifices are offered (1 Kgs 11:7; 2 Kgs 23:10; Jer 32:35).[32] Otto Eißfeldt, in his study *Molk als Opferbegriff* (1935), showed that no deity Molek ever existed, and in fact the Hebrew word is a technical sacrificial term, a cognate of Punic **molk*. In the Hebrew Bible, children are sacrificed "for a *mulk* offering" (*lam-mōlek*) to Yahweh.[33] In the Deuteronomistic History, Molek is a

---

recognizes deuteronomistic polemic at work when the asherah/Asherah is associated with the cult of Baal; in the Bible, Asherah seems to be a goddess "plus ou moins parèdre de Baal. . . . Cependant ces textes se rattachent à la rédaction deutéronomiste qui, pour mieux extirper le culte des *ashérîm* les associe au culte de Baal et enfait des idoles étrangères au Yahvisme." ("Les inscriptions," 606 n.54).

[30] We shall argue this in depth in Chapter 3.

[31] Cross, *Canaanite Myth* 73-75, 197-200.

[32] Human sacrifice is also prohibited in the Priestly materials. See Lev 18:21; 20:2, 3, 4.

[33] Eißfeldt, *Molk als Opferbegriff im Punischen und Hebräischen und das Ende des Gottes Moloch* (Halle: Niemeyer, 1935). He argues (1) that Punic *mlk* (Latin transcription *molc*) and Hebrew *mōlek* were cognate terms of sacrifice, and (2) that

god of the Ammonites (1 Kings 11:7). Let us say for the sake of argument that the deuteronomistic writers actually believed that humans were being sacrificed to a foreign god Molek in Israel. Even if this were the case, Jer 32:35 indicates very clearly that willful confusion is being employed, because here, human sacrifice (*mōlek*) is associated with Baal, and nowhere in Canaanite religion do we find this. Human sacrifice, as we shall discuss, is the province of El, both in Sanchuniathon and in the Punic world of the late first millennium.[34] But this deuteronomistic prose editorial text from Jeremiah claims that *bāmôt* were built for Baal in the Valley of ben Hinnom where human

children in Israel were sacrificed to Yahweh, not a foreign god Molek. There is no doubt that *mulk/milk* is also a divine title in certain contexts. *PE* 1.10.44 emphasizes the royal nature of El's sacrifice of his own son. In a recent study, G.C. Heider rejects Eißfeldt's thesis and reasserts a new version of the traditional view. He argues that Molek was a chthonic deity worshiped in the cult of the dead (*The Cult of Molek: A Reassessment* [Journal for the Study of the Old Testament Supplements 43; Sheffield: Journal for the Study of the Old Testament, 1986]). We do not find this argument convincing in light of the comparative evidence and in light of the deuteronomistic tendency toward polemical distortion. Heider does not succeed in demonstrating that a god Molek or Malik ever existed in any cult. See our review (with M.S. Smith) of Heider's monograph in *RB* 94 (1987) 273-75. M. Weinfeld ("The Worship of Moloch and the Queen of Heaven," *UF* 4 [1972] 133-54) argues that children were never really burned. His arguments are most unconvincing.

[34] The cult of human sacrifice is closely associated with El in extant texts from the first millennium. According to Sanchuniathon, El sacrificed his "only" son in royal attire when war threatened the land (*PE* 1.10.44). The son is called *Ieoud, Idoud* or *Iedod* in some variant texts. This seems to reflect **yahîd*, "only son" or **yadîd*, "beloved." See the comments of H.W. Attridge and R. Oden, *Philo of Byblos: The Phoenician History* (CBQMS 9; Washington: Catholic Biblical Association, 1981) 94 n.150. In another fragment, El sacrifices his "only son" (*monogenē huion*, reflecting **yahîd*) to his father Ouranos during a plague (*PE* 1.10.33-34). Punic Baal Hamon, who is to be identified with El (according to our arguments ahead), accepted human sacrifices. See the discussions of Albright, *Yahweh and the Gods of Canaan* (Garden City: Doubleday, 1968) 236-43, and Cross, *Canaanite Myth* 24-28. Albright (*Archaeology and the Religion of Israel* 162-64) criticized Eißfeldt's arguments concerning the *mulk* sacrifice. He believed that there was a deity Molek, though he later reversed his views (see *Yahweh and the Gods of Canaan* 236). Albright pointed out that there was, in the Aramean and north Mesopotamian sphere, a connection between the god Adad and human sacrifice (*Yahweh and the Gods of Canaan* 240; *Archaeology and the Religion of Israel* 221 n.116b). He believed that the Arameans were the source of such sacrifices in Israel from the time of Ahaz on. There is little evidence to support this view, since human sacrifice was long established in Canaanite religion. It seems quite evident that human sacrifices to Yahweh were an indigenous practice in certain Israelite circles. Though human sacrifices to Adad are attested outside of the Canaanite sphere, nowhere are they attested within it. Human sacrifice in Canaanite religion was the province of El. Thus it seems likely that the association of Baal with the tophet of Jerusalem is simply polemical, unless we are to posit an Aramean-style Adad cult in sixth-century Jerusalem. See our discussion of Adrammelek in Chapter 4.

sacrifices were performed. In this text, *lammōlek* can be read "for a *mulk* offering": *wayyibnû 'et-bāmôt habba'al 'ăšer*[35] *bĕgê' ben-hinnōm lĕha'ăbîr 'et-bĕnêhem wĕ'et-bĕnôtêhem lammōlek 'ăšer lō'-ṣiwwitîm wĕlō' 'ālĕtâ 'al-libbî la'ăśôt hattô'ēbâ hazzō't lĕma'an haḥăṭî' 'et-yĕhûdâ*, "And they built the high places of Baal which are in the Valley of ben Hinnom in order to cause their sons and daughters to pass through [the fire] for a human sacrifice though I did not command them, nor did it enter my mind, to do this abomination, causing Judah to transgress." In this text, deuteronomistic polemic has associated human sacrifice with the cult of Baal. Jer 19:5 is similar. Yet it is interesting to note that behind the superficial association of human sacrifice with Baal is a clear allusion to such sacrifices being given to Yahweh: "though I did not command them, nor did it enter my mind." This expression is always used of practices dedicated to Yahweh which the deuteronomists oppose. In fact, Jer 7:31 uses the same expression in a context where it is clear that sacrifices to Yahweh are meant: "And they built high places, the tophet which is in the Valley of ben Hinnom, in order to burn their sons and their daughters in fire, which I did not command nor did it enter my mind. . . ." This association of child sacrifice with Yahweh's cult is evident in several other passages from the Prophets. In Mic 6:6-7, sacrifice of the firstborn child for the transgression of the parent is listed with other excessive forms of sacrifice to Yahweh (thousands of rams, rivers of oil) which are unnecessary according to the prophet. Micah does not condemn child sacrifice per se as immoral, "foreign," or "Canaanite;" it is simply not what Yahweh wants. He wants justice and covenant-loyalty. In Isa 30:33, the precinct for human sacrifices (*tōpet*) has been prepared, and Yahweh's breath "like a stream of brimstone" kindles the pyre. The expression *lammelek*, "for the king," if original to the text, should be emended to *lammōlek* "for the human sacrifice."[36] Ezek 20:25-26, 31 is another witness to human sacrifices offered to Yahweh. In light of the evidence, the case for a cult in Israel dedicated to a god Molek is exceedingly weak. Eißfeldt's arguments remain convincing.

Based only on an examination of the biblical sources, we argue that the asherah was a legitimate part of the cult of Yahweh both in the north and in the south, in state religion and in popular religion, finding opposition in deuteronomistic circles. We

[35] Syr adds **bĕtōpet*.
[36] See n.33 on Heider and our review (with M.S. Smith).

suggest that the association of Asherah and her symbol with Baal is the result of a deuteronomistic polemic against the asherah in Yahweh's cult. What better way to give the cult symbol the stamp of Yahwistic illegitimacy than to associate it with Baal and his cult?

The asherah is mentioned four times in the prophetic corpus (three time with altars): Jer 17:2; Isa 17:8; 27:9 and Mic 5:13 (Eng. 14). We shall now examine each passage in some depth. All seem to show either deuteronomistic influence or provenance. This can be determined by an analysis of the language of each passage as well as its theology.

(1) Jer 17:2: *kizkōr běnêhem mizběḥôtām wa'ăšērêhem 'al-'ēṣ ra'ănān 'al gěbā'ôt haggěbōhôt*, "while their children remember their altars and their asherahs under the green tree(s) and upon the high hills. . . ." The close relationship of the book of Jeremiah to deuteronomistic circles has been much discussed, and disputed by some.[37] It is difficult to accept the arguments of those who see no relationship between at least the prose sections of Jeremiah and the deuteronomistic school. The linguistic and theological affinities are striking. In the prose section under consideration, the telling cliché high hills/green trees occurs (in a modified form with the order hills/trees reversed).[38] This expression is very common throughout the deuteronomistic corpus, strongly suggesting the deuteronomistic provenance of

---

[37] See M. Weinfeld, *Deuteronomy and the Deuteronomic School* (Oxford: Clarendon, 1972) 359-61; J. Bright, *Jeremiah* (AB 21; Garden City: Doubleday, 1965) lxvii-lxxiii, for discussion and bibliography, as well as Bright, "The Date of the Prose Sermons of Jeremiah," *JBL* 70 (1951) 15-35; J.P. Hyatt, "Jeremiah and Deuteronomy," *JNES* 1 (1942) 156-73; and the earlier work of S. Mowinckel, *Zur Komposition des Buches Jeremia* (Oslo: Dybwad, 1914). Though most scholars would agree that there is a close relationship between the prose sections of Jeremiah and the writings of the deuteronomistic school, this view has been challenged recently by H. Weippert, *Die Prosareden des Jeremiabuches* (Berlin: De Gruyter, 1973). We see little reason to doubt such a close relationship. R. Pratt, in an unpublished paper entitled "Controversy in Exile," (Harvard University, 1984) argues persuasively that a particular group of exilic deuteronomists, which he calls JDtr, edited the Jeremiah material, but their theology can be characterized as an optimistic response to exile, a reaction to the pessimism of the Dtr₂ circle.

[38] Compare Deut 12:2, *'al-haggěbā'ôt wětaḥat kol-'ēṣ ra'ănān* and 2 Kgs 17:10, *'al kol-gib'â gěbōhâ wětaḥat kol-'ēṣ ra'ănān*. Jer 17:2 reverses the order hill(s)//tree(s) and uses the preposition *'al* instead of *taḥat*. The expression occurs elsewhere in the Deuteronomistic History (1 Kgs 14:23; 2 Kgs 16:4; Jer 2:20; 3:6). See also Isa 57:5, where this expression occurs, reflecting deuteronomistic influence on Trito-Isaiah. Alleged non-Yahwistic worship is always the context in which this expression occurs. W. Holladay ("On Every High Hill and Under Every Green Tree," *VT* 11 [1961] 170-76) argues that the expression stems originally from Hos 4:13.

this passage. The concern for sanctuaries outside of Jerusalem usually suggests deuteronomistic influence or provenance, and the mention of altars in the country here is no exception. Note that the cult under consideration here is that of Yahweh outside of Jerusalem. Nowhere is Baal mentioned. The shorter text of LXX is lacking this verse; vv 2-3a read like a gloss.

(2) Isa 17:7-8: *bayyôm hahû' yiš'eh hā'ādām 'al-'ōśēhû wĕ'ênāyw 'el-qĕdôš yiśrā'ēl tir'ênâ wĕlō' yiš'eh 'el-hammizbĕḥôt ma'ăśēh yādāyw wa'ăšer 'āśû 'eṣbĕ'ôtāyw lō' yir'eh wĕhā'ăšērîm wĕhāḥammānîm*, "On that day, humans will look upon him that made them, and their eyes will look to Israel's Holy One. They will no longer look to the altars, the work of their hands, and they will have no more regard for what their fingers have made [that is, the asherahs and the incense altars]." These two verses may be an addition to the oracle against Damascus, reflecting deuteronomistic language and theology ("the works of their hands," concern for altars).[39] The last two words (asherahs and incense altars) read awkwardly like a later editorial gloss on the text and are certainly of deuteronomistic provenance.[40]

(3) Isa 27:9: *lākēn bĕzō't yĕkuppar 'ăwôn-ya'ăqōb// wĕzeh kol-pĕrî hāsîr ḥaṭṭā'tô// bĕśûmô kol-'abnê mizbēaḥ// kĕ 'abnê-gīr mĕnuppāṣôt// lō'-yāqūmû 'ăšērîm wĕhammānîm*, "Thus by this the guilt of Jacob will be expiated// And this will be the full fruit of the removal of his transgression:// When he makes every stone of the altar// Like stones of chalk shattered// [And] the asherahs and incense altars stand no longer." Asherahs and altars are again mentioned in the context of Jacob's sin/guilt. Some of the same expressions occur here as in Isa 17:7-8 (the pairing of *'ăšērîm* and *ḥammānîm*, and the mention of the *mizbēaḥ*). As in Jer 17:2, transgression is the issue, but Baal is not mentioned. The passage is a part of the Isaianic

---

[39] The expression "the work of x's hands" (*ma'ăśēh yādāyw* here) is another common deuteronomistic cliché, often used in reference to illegitimate or non-Yahwistic cultic practices (Deut 4:28; 27:15; 2 Kgs 22:17). Weinfeld (*Deuteronomy* 324) believes that this term, when used for idols, also stems originally from Hosea (4:14).
[40] Wilderberger (*Jesaja 13-27*, 637) recognizes *hammizbĕḥôt* and *hā'ăšērîm wĕhammānîm* as glosses. This is a common scholarly opinion. Wilderberger, however, does not recognize the deuteronomistic background of the expression *ma'ăśēh yādāyw*, but relates it to "creation theology" (651). This is not incorrect, but the context itself (at least the end of v 8 where altars and the asherah are mentioned) suggests a deuteronomistic provenance, and this is what is significant. See also O. Kaiser, *Der Prophet Jesaja, Kapitel 13-39* (ATD 18; Göttingen: Vandenhoeck & Ruprecht, 1973) 66-67. Deuteronomistic editing of the book of Isaiah is not disputed. See chapters 36-39, paralleling approximately 2 Kgs 18-20.

Apocalypse (Isaiah 24-27), to be dated to the exilic period and attributed to "Trito-Isaiah" (the school of Deutero-Isaiah).[41] The concerns of this passage are close to those of the deuteronomistic school (altars, asherahs, guilt/sin of Jacob). The relationship of the school of Second Isaiah and the deuteronomistic school needs to be explored in more depth. In Isa 57:3-5, there is concern for transgression (*yildê-pešaʿ*) and child sacrifice, and the deuteronomistic expression *taḥat kol-ʿēṣ raʿănān* ("Under every luxuriant tree") occurs (v 5). This text, like Isa 27:9, suggests that deuteronomistic theology and language had an influence on "Third Isaiah."[42] The influence may be due simply to the generalization of the deuteronomistic polemic in the exilic and post-exilic periods. It may no longer be the view of a single circle by this time.

(4) Mic 5:13: The oracle collection of Micah 4-5 alludes to a siege (4:14) and the emergence of a Davidic king (5:1-3). The Assyrians are mentioned by name in vv 4-5, and there is an allusion to cult reform, in which the asherahs are mentioned, in vv 9-13. All of this suggests a dating to the time between Hezekiah's cultic reform and the Assyrian investment of Jerusalem (701). The oracle concerning cult reform may have been uttered by Micah in order to support Hezekiah's efforts.[43] Hezekiah's reform and centralization of the cult was carried out along deuteronomistic lines, as some scholars have pointed

[41] P.D. Hanson ("Apocalypticism," *IDBSup* 33) identifies Isaiah 24-27 as literature related to the apocalyptic movement of the late sixth and the fifth centuries, along with Isaiah 34-35; 56-66; Malachi; Zechariah 9-14. See also G. Fohrer, "Die Aufbau der Apokalypse des Jesajabuchs (ls. 24-27)," *CBQ* 25 (1963) 34-45; B. Otzen, "Traditions and Structures of Isaiah xxiv-xxvii," *VT* 24 (1974) 196-211; J. Lindblom, *Die Jesaja-Apokalypse, Jes. 24-27* (Lund: Gleerup, 1938); W. Millar, *Isaiah 24-27 and the Origin of Apocalyptic* (HSM 11; Missoula, MT: Scholars, 1976).

[42] W. Brueggemann ("Isaiah 55 and Deuteronomic Theology," *ZAW* 80 [1968] 191-203) argues that Deutero-Isaiah and the deuteronomistic school (his "historian") shared "theological motifs" and that Deutero-Isaiah is most closely related to Dtr of all his contemporaries or near contemporaries.

[43] This has been argued persuasively by J.T. Willis, "The Authenticity and Meaning of Micah 5:9-14," *ZAW* 81 (1969) 353-68. He states that "5:9-14 fits well historically in the time of Micah as an oracle delivered by an eighth-century prophet to stimulate the reform of Hezekiah" (367). D. Hillers (*Micah* [Hermeneia; Philadelphia: Fortress, 1984] 73-74) doubts this assertion "in detail," citing the critique of horses and chariots in v 9 as something not included in Hezekiah's reform program. Yet this criticism is weak at best. As Willis himself pointed out, it is characteristic of prophets to criticize those who depend not on Yahweh but on human might (Isa 31:1-3; Amos 2:13-16; Hos 8:14). J. Blenkinsopp (*A History of Prophecy in Israel* [Philadelphia: Westminster, 1983] 120) argues for a later date for chaps. 4-5. The material in chap. 4 does not seem to predate the material in chap. 5.

out.[44] In this passage, the sorceries (kĕšāpîm), soothsayers (mĕʿ ônĕnîm), idols (pĕsîlêkā), pillars (maṣṣĕbôtêkā) and asherahs are to be cut off (hikrattî). Compare Deut 16:21-22; 18:10-12. The deuteronomistic expression maʿ ăśēh yādêkā occurs in v 12b.[45] This oracle, if it is authentic to Micah, indicates that he was profoundly influenced by deuteronomistic thought. Perhaps he was a member of the deuteronomistic school. In any case, the passage mentioning the asherahs shows signs of deuteronomistic influence, even provenance.

Our survey of the four places in the prophetic corpus where the asherah is mentioned suggests strongly that these texts are either of deuteronomistic provenance (Jer 17:2; Isa 17:8), or betray the influence of deuteronomistic language and theology (Isa 27:9; Mic 5:13). There is no mention of the asherah in Hosea and Amos, and it would seem that the Elijah-Elisha school did not oppose it. This is indeed striking. The evidence suggests that no prophet (whose traditions are extant) opposed the asherah, except for those subject to deuteronomistic influence. It is equally worth noting that in the four passages we have just considered, nowhere is Baal mentioned. The cults under criticism are all Yahwistic, probably those of the outlying sanctuaries.

[44] H.W. Wolff (Dodekapropheton Micha [BKAT 14/12-14; Neukirchen-Vluyn: Neukirchener, 1980-82] 132-33) has argued for the presence of deuteronomistic thought in this passage (Micah 5), and pointed out that the root NTŠ is characteristic of Dtr-Jer (Deut 29:27; 1 Kgs 14:15; Jer 12:14; Amos 9:15, all with reference to exile. In Mic 5:13 it is used of the asherah). Some scholars believe that vv 13-14 (or only v 14) are a gloss on Micah's oracle. Wolff (132-35) separates vv 9-12 from vv 13-14, and A. Weiser (Die Propheten Hosea, Joel, Amos, Obadja, Jona, Micha [ATD 24; Göttingen: Vandenhoeck & Ruprecht, 1974] 278) thinks vv 9-13 are an original unit. Weinfeld (Deuteronomy 163-64) discusses the relationship of the deuteronomistic school to Hezekiah's reform. See also J. Rosenbaum, "Hezekiah's Reform and the Deuteronomistic Tradition," HTR 72 (1979) 23-43; N. Lohfink, "Deuteronomy," IDBSup 231. Evidence from Tel Arad shows that the altars of burnt offerings were removed in the time of Hezekiah (level VIII), and the temple, which had been destroyed, was rebuilt without them (VII). After a second destruction of the temple in the era of Josiah (VI), it was not rebuilt. Lohfink: "thus, we can differentiate between an abolition of sacrifices outside Jerusalem under Hezekiah and a destruction of the sanctuaries themselves under Josiah. In that case, the essence of the Deuteronomic laws of centralization should be attributed to Hezekiah rather than Josiah" (231). See Y. Aharoni, "Arad: Its Inscriptions and Temple," BA 31 (1968) 18-32, especially 26-27.

[45] See n.39. The full expression in Mic 5:12 is wĕlōʾ tištaḥăweh ʿ ôd lĕmaʿ ăśēh yādêkā. Micah here seems to have combined two separate deuteronomistic expressions, maʿ ăśēh yād- and hištaḥăwâ. For the latter, see Weinfeld, Deuteronomy 321 #4, #5a, #6, #7. In Deut 4:28, the verb ʿBD is used with maʿ ăśēh yād- in reference to idols. Blenkinsopp (History 122-23) believes Micah influenced the deuteronomists.

Outside of the Deuteronomistic History and the prophetic corpus, there are a number of passages that mention the asherah. The first we shall consider is Exod 34:13-14: *kî 'et-mizbĕḥōtām tittōṣûn wĕ'et-maṣṣēbōtām tĕšabbĕrûn wĕ'et-'ăšērāyw tikrōtûn kî lō' tištaḥăweh lĕ'ēl 'aḥēr kî Yahweh qannā' šĕmô 'ēl qannā' hû'*, "For their altars you shall tear down, and their pillars you shall shatter, and their asherahs you shall cut down, for you shall not prostrate yourselves to another god, for Yahweh the jealous one is his name, he is a jealous God." Though the context of this passage is the so-called Yahwistic decalogue, the language and concerns of vv 11-13, 15-16 are deuteronomistic in provenance. This has been argued by a number of scholars who have commented on the passage.[46] We argue that v 14 is probably original to the passage (*kî lō' tištaḥăweh lĕ'ēl 'aḥēr kî Yahweh qannā' šĕmô 'ēl qannā' hû'*). A comparison of v 13 with Deut 12:3 illustrates its deuteronomistic background: *wĕnittaṣtem 'et-mizbĕḥōtām wĕšibbartem 'et-maṣṣēbōtām wa'ăšērêhem tiśrĕpûn bā'ēš.* The only difference between the two passages is the cutting down/burning with fire contrast for the asherahs. Otherwise, they are virtually identical.

Aside from the passages discussed, there remain only the eleven passages in Chronicles where the asherah is mentioned, and of these, eight are taken from the Chronicler's *Vorlage* of the Deuteronomistic History. This leaves only 2 Chr 17:6 and its expansion in 19:3, and 2 Chr 24:18, texts with no parallel in the Deuteronomistic History. In 2 Chronicles 17 material about the reign of Jehoshaphat is found. Included is the claim that he undertook a cultic reform, removing the high places and the asherahs. 2 Chr 24:18 comments on the disloyalty of Judah to Yahweh after the death of Jehoiada, mentioning asherahs and idols. These passages, which have no deuteronomistic parallels, reflect the influence of the deuteronomistic polemic against asherahs, high places and so on, though they occur in the Chronicler's work. After all, the Chronicler made extensive use of deuteronomistic source material in his construction of Israel's history. Eight other passages that criticize the asherah, all from deuteronomistic source material, were incorporated into the

---

[46] B. Childs, *The Book of Exodus: A Critical Theological Commentary* (Old Testament Library; Philadelphia: Westminster, 1974) 608-609. M. Noth (*Exodus* [Old Testament Library; Philadelphia: Westminster, 1962] 262) argues that vv 11b-13, 14b-16 are deuteronomistic additions. Verse 14a is original and belongs with the preceding material.

Chronicler's work.[47] The best explanation remains the one offered previously: by the time of the exile and restoration, the
anti-Asherah polemic had become generalized, and was no
longer associated only with a single circle.

There is no direct condemnation of the asherah in Hosea,
though some scholars have argued that 4:12 and 14:9 allude to it
in such a manner.[48] In both passages there are difficulties in arguing that the asherah is meant, and in neither case is the word
asherah found. In light of the fact that both passages can be interpreted without reference to the asherah, it seems unlikely
that it is intended. The MT of Hos 4:12 reads: ʿammî bĕʿēṣô
yišʾāl// ûmaqlô yaggîd lô, "My people inquire of their [his]
wooden thing"// "And their [his] staff gives them [him] oracles." H.W. Wolff, D.N. Freedman and F. Anderson, and Biblia
Hebraica Stuttgartensia (among others) read with LXX, seeing
the priest as the subject of v 12, and "my people" as part of the
object of the previous colon (kardia laou mou, *lēb ʿammî)
which has been displaced.[49] Thus, "He (the priest) inquires of
his wooden thing"// "And his staff gives him oracles."[50] Scholars have debated the meaning of this. The noun ʿēṣ may be ambiguous when it stands alone, but in this case the B term maqqēl
clarifies what is intended in the verse. A rod or stick of some

---

[47] The Chronicler utilized a Dtr Vorlage when he constructed his work. S. McKenzie, in his monograph The Chronicler's Use of the Deuteronomistic History (HSM
33; Chico, CA: Scholars, 1985), argues that the Chronicler made use of a proto-
rabbinic Vorlage of Kings. On the dating of Chr 1, or the first edition of the Chronicler's work, see D.N. Freedman, "The Chronicler's Purpose," CBQ 23 (1961) 436-
42, where he argues that the first edition is to be dated to the time of Zerubbabel.
See further F.M. Cross, "A Reconstruction of the Judean Restoration," Int 29 (1975)
187-202 = JBL 94 (1975) 4-18.

[48] J. Day, "A Case of Inner Scriptural Interpretation," JTS 31 (1980) 309-19, especially 314-15. H.W. Wolff (Hosea [Hermeneia; Philadelphia: Fortress, 1974] 237)
thinks that the metaphor of 14:9 (Yahweh as a fruit-bearing tree) has a polemical
intent: "Once again Hosea's polemical theology—[is] now in dispute with the trees
and oracles of the Canaanite cult. . . . In contrast to the syncretism of Canaanite
religion, Hosea declares that the fertility and vitality Ephraim vainly sought in its
Canaanite cult is to be found in his god alone." This, we presume, means that Wolff
sees an allusion to the asherah in this passage, though this is not stated. See also T.
Robinson in F. Horst and T. Robinson, Die Zwölfkleinen Propheten (HAT 1/4; Tübingen: Mohr, 1964) 19-20.

[49] F. Andersen and D.N. Freedman, Hosea (AB 24; Garden City: Doubleday, 1980)
343. Wolff, ibid. 72.

[50]   LXX: [11]porneian kai oinon kai methysma
                edexato kardia laou mou
                [12]en symbolois epērōtōn, kai en rhabdois
                autou apēngellon autōi

sort must be involved.[51] A graven image or a tree (either living or stylized) is not intended here. The noun *maqqēl* never refers to a tree, only a rod or staff, or a tree branch used as a staff.[52] The *'ēṣ* must have a similar meaning in this passage. The use of the idiom *S'L B-*, "to inquire of," suggests divination of some kind.[53] See Deut 18:11 *šō'ēl 'ōb*, a type of diviner, and 1 Chr 10:13, where the idiom is used in the context of Saul's visit to the medium (*wĕgam-liš'ōl bā'ōb. . .*).[54] In light of the use of the idiom *S'L B-* and the parallelism *'ēṣ*//*maqqēl*, it is probable that Hos 4:12 alludes to cultic rhabdomancy, or the casting of sticks by the priest to obtain oracles. Belomancy is also possible but less likely.[55] It seems far less plausible that we have here an allusion to divination by a tree, a statue or an asherah.[56] If the asherah were meant, one would expect the word to occur here. There is no evidence in this passage that any non-Yahwistic cult is intended. Certainly 4:6a and 12b suggest that the priest serves Yahweh.

Hos 14:9 (English 8) has been mentioned in connection with Asherah and her cultic symbol. It reads: *'eprayim mah-lô*[57] *'ôd lā 'ăṣabbîm*// *'ănî 'ānîtî wă'ăšûrennû*// *'ănî kibrôš ra'ănān*// *mimmennî peryĕkā nimṣā'*, "As for Ephraim, what interest should he have with idols any more?// I, indeed, have answered

---

[51] Andersen and Freedman note this (*Hosea* 365). H.L. Ginsberg, ("Lexicographical Notes," in *Hebräische Wortforschung. Festschrift zum 80. Geburtstag von Walter Baumgartner* [VTSup 16; Leiden: Brill, 1967] 74-75) argues that the two terms suggest "penis." We see no evidence in the text to support this interpretation. Andersen and Freedman think that the *'ēṣ* and *maqqēl* symbolize a deity (366), but again this is not substantiated by the passage. Note that the priest is a servant of Yahweh (vv 6a, 12b).

[52] Wolff (*Hosea*, 84) states that it is impossible to say whether or not the *'ēṣ* here is an asherah, an oracular tree, or something related to the teraphim. W. Rudolph (*Hosea* [KAT 13/1; Gütersloh: Mohn, 1966] 110) notes the ambiguity of the two terms, as do Weiser (*Die Propheten* 47-48) and W. Nowack (*Die kleinen Propheten* [Göttingen Handkommentar zum Alten Testament 3/4; Göttingen: Vandenhoeck & Ruprecht, 1922] 33). We feel that a word study of *maqqēl* helps considerably to narrow the range of possibilities. The text is not as ambiguous as some scholars have maintained.

[53] Wolff, *Hosea* 84 notes this, citing Judg 1:1 and 2 Sam 2:1, as do Andersen and Freedman, *Hosea* 365.

[54] *lidrōš* here is redundant, and missing from Syr. Thus we have chosen to delete. On the *'ōb* and its general Semitic background, see H.A. Hoffner, "Second Millennium Antecedents to the Hebrew *'ōb*," *JBL* 86 (1967) 385-401, and "*'ôbh*," *TDOT* 1:130-34. Both the *'ōb* and the teraphim are connected to the underworld.

[55] I. Mendelsohn ("Divination," *IDB* 1:858) and B.O. Long, ("Divination," *IDBSup* 24) mention the possibility of belomancy for this passage.

[56] Against Andersen and Freedman, *Hosea* 366.

[57] Here we read with LXX (*autōi*, **lô*), instead of MT *lî*, "to me."

and watched over him.// I am like a luxuriant cypress// From me your fruit is found." Wellhausen suggested that *'ănî 'ănîtî wă'ăśûrennû* be emended to *'ănî 'ănātô wa'ăśērātô*, "I am his Anat and his Asherah," a fanciful and unfounded emendation.[58] In this text, Yahweh is the luxuriant cypress of Israel, from which all good things come. The simile should not occasion surprise. It seems unlikely that Anat or Asherah is even suggested here, let alone mentioned, though such an allusion has been argued by some scholars.[59]

John Day argued recently that Hos 14:9 (as well as 4:12) is to be seen as an anti-asherah polemic: "In particular it would seem that Hos. xiv.9 (English 8) is condemning the Asherim, the poles sacred to the goddess Asherah. . . ."[60] Yet the luxuriant cypress of Hos 14:9 is clearly Yahweh. Ironically, Day himself is convinced that the asherah is never a living tree, but this tree in Hos 14:9 is described as "luxuriant," bearing fruit. Thus, he contradicts himself. Day accepts Wolff's view that this passage alludes to "Canaanite" cult practices in a polemical manner, and this we reject. It in no way suggests Asherah or her symbol. The only possible allusion to "Canaanite" practices is *'ăṣăbbîm* (idols). Even if Day is correct in seeing Isa 27:9 as an interpretation of Hos 14:9 (this is possible but there are problems), the mention of asherahs in Isa 27:9 suggests only that the author of Isa 27:9 understood Hos 14:9 in this way, not that this is what was originally intended by Hos 14:9. The mention of the asherahs in Isa 27:9 can be explained by deuteronomistic influence. Concern for altars (*mizbēaḥ, ḥammānîm*), asherahs, and sin/guilt ('*āwôn, ḥaṭṭā't*), suggests this, but these are not present in Hos 14:9. In 14:9, only idols ('*ăṣabbîm*) are mentioned, and these are not found in the Isaiah passage. The fact that each passage has different concerns casts doubt on Day's thesis. Is the Isaiah passage truly an interpretation of Hos 14:9?

There is no mention of the asherah in Hosea, nor is there an allusion to it in 4:12 or 14:9. This is interesting in light of the probable linguistic and theological affinities between Hosea and

---

[58] *Die kleinen Propheten* (3rd ed.; Berlin: Reimer, 1898) 134. Wellhausen is followed by G. Fohrer ("Umkehr und Erlösung beim Propheten Hosea," *TZ* 11 (1955) 171 and n.18), E. Jacob (Jacob, C.A. Keller, and A. Amsler, *Osée, Joël, Amos, Abdias, Jonas* [CAT 11a; Neuchâtel: Delachaux & Niestlé, 1965] 95, 97), and recently Weinfeld, "Kuntillet 'Ajrud," 122-23.

[59] It is a common assertion that at least Asherah, if not Anat, is suggested in this passage both by the mention of the luxuriant tree and by *'ănî' 'ănîtî wa'ăśûrennû*. See for example, Day, "A Case of Inner Scriptural Interpretation," 315, and "Asherah," 405.

[60] Ibid. 314.

the writings of the deuteronomistic school, which M. Weinfeld
has argued reflect "a current of northern thought flowing down
to Judah, following the fall of Samaria."[61] In Hosea, there is severe condemnation of the cult of Baal, and critique of the maṣṣēbôt, the calf of Bethel, the high places and altars.[62] These
concerns are similar to those of the deuteronomistic school. Yet
why is there no mention of the asherah in Hosea, especially if
there is a close relationship to the theology and language of the
deuteronomistic school? In deuteronomistic narratives, the
asherah is a central concern. Weinfeld does not discuss this
problem. If we are correct in our interpretation of Hos 4:12 and
14:9, we can suggest that the opposition to the asherah and
Asherah is a deuteronomistic innovation. This of course assumes
that the deuteronomistic school was influenced by Hosea, and
not vice versa. There is no evidence that the asherah was opposed by anyone in Israel before the reforming kings, who were
following a deuteronomistic program, as scholars generally
recognize.

---

[61] *Deuteronomy* 366. See also A. Alt, "Die Heimat des Deuteronomiums," in
Kleine Schriften zur Geschichte des Volkes Israel (Munich: Becksche, 1953) 2:250-
75, especially 270-75.
[62] (a) maṣṣēbâ/-ôt: 3:4; 10:1, 2; (b) bāmôt: 10:8 (nišmĕdû bāmôt 'āwen// ḥaṭṭā't
yiśrā'ēl); (c) mizbĕḥôt: 10:1, 2, 8. The asherah is nowhere mentioned, and this is
striking.

Chapter 2

EPIGRAPHIC SOURCES PERTAINING TO THE CULT OF ASHERAH

The second chapter of this study will consist of an examination of the relevant epigraphic data. The asherah (or less likely, Asherah) is mentioned several times in the inscriptions from Kuntillet Ajrûd (Horvat Teman, 50 km south of Kadesh Barnea), and is probably mentioned in the tomb inscription from Khirbet el-Qôm, a site in Judah between Lachish and Hebron. We shall begin with the evidence of el-Qôm inscription 3.[1] There has been much debate over the reading of this text.[2] Based on paleographic considerations, it is to be dated to the end of the eighth century (ca. 700). The writing is very close to that of the Siloam tunnel inscription from Jerusalem. The earlier date (ca. 750), proposed by W. Dever in the *editio princeps* and accepted by A. Lemaire, is less likely.[3]

Most scholars agree that line two of the inscription is to be read *brk 'ryhw lyhwh*. Z. Zevit, in a recent contribution to the discussion, reads *brkt*, based on analysis of new photographs, slides and examination of the inscription under various lighting conditions.[4] If Zevit's reading *brkt* is accepted, one can vocalize **barriktī 'ūrīyahû la-yahweh*, "I bless Uriyahu by Yahweh." Otherwise, one could read *brk*, "Uriyahu is blessed by Yahweh" (**burrak*, the pual perfect, or **barūk*, the qal passive participle). In any case the meaning is not affected.

---

[1] The *editio princeps* is W. Dever, "Iron Age Epigraphic Material from the Area of Khirbet el-Kôm," *HUCA* 40/41 (1970) 139-204.

[2] The various views of scholars are summarized nicely in Z. Zevit, "The Khirbet el-Qôm Inscription Mentioning a Goddess," *BASOR* 255 (1984) 39-47. See Dever, ibid.; A. Lemaire, "Les inscriptions," 597-608; "Who or What was Yahweh's Asherah?" *Biblical Archaeology Review* 10.6 (1984) 42-51; S. Mittmann, "Die Grabinschrift des Sängers Uriahu," *ZDPV* 97 (1981) 139-52; J. Naveh, "Graffiti and Dedications," *BASOR* 235 (1979) 27-30.

[3] F.M. Cross suggested the date circa 700. For the views of Dever, see ibid. 165, and for those of Lemaire, "Les inscriptions," 603.

[4] Ibid. 39-40, 43. On the common blessing formula, see B. Couroyer, "*BRK* et les formules égyptiennes de salutation," *RB* 85 (1978) 575-85, and D. Pardee, "Letters from Tel Arad," *UF* 10 (1978) 311.

Line three is far more difficult, both to read and to interpret. There is much disagreement concerning even its reading, and therefore caution is warranted in its analysis. Lemaire, now supported by several others including Zevit, read *wmṣryh l'šrth hwš'lh* after the removal of various extra letters inscribed in a run-on fashion in the line (Zevit: *wm̊mṣrryyh/r hl'lš'rttrhhwš'lh*).[5] Zevit would translate "and from his enemies" for *wmṣryh*, following Lemaire, but there are difficulties with this. The *he* is an uncertain reading, as Zevit himself notes. The proposed suffix -*yh* (3 ms on a plural noun) is at best an unusual and unexpected form. In pre-exilic epigraphic Hebrew, the expected 3 ms suffix for a plural noun is -*w*, as in Lachish 3.18 *'nšw* (**'anašaw*, "his men").[6] If -*yh* is not a suffix, and we frankly doubt that it is, what then would *wmṣryh/r*(?) mean? J. Naveh reads *nṣry*, "my guardian," and this is certainly a possibility.[7] Thus, "May Uriyahu be blessed by Yahweh my guardian." Because of the uncertain nature of the text here, we prefer to pass over this word. At the end of the line, the imperative *hwš'lh* (**hawši'luh*), "deliver him," seems clear enough. But what about *l'šrth*? If one follows Zevit's reading (*hl'lš'rttrh*) the text is wholly uncertain here, though it is possible that *l'šrth* is intended. Lemaire, reading *wmṣryh l'šrth hwš'lh*, argued that *l'šrth*, "his asherah", must be moved before *wmṣryh*, claiming that the engraver had erred in determining the order of the words when he wrote the inscription. Thus, "Béni soit Uryahu par Yhwh et par son ashérah."[8] Lemaire's interesting sugges-

---

[5] Zevit reads *wm̊mṣrryyh/r hl'lš'rttrhhwš'lh* (ibid. 43). Others who follow Lemaire's reading of the text (without his emendation) are J.R. Engle, "Pillar Figurines of Iron Age Israel and Asherah-Asherim," (Ph.D. dissertation, University of Pittsburgh, 1979) 82, and K. Jaroš, "Zur Inschrift Nr. 3 von Hirbet el-Qôm," *Biblische Notizen* 19 (1982) 30-41.

[6] See also *yrḥw* (**yarḥêw*), "his two months," of the Gezer Calendar (*KAI* 182), a 3ms suffix on a dual noun (**-ayhu > *-êhu > *-êw*, through contraction of the diphthong **-ay > *-ê*, and syncope of intervocalic *he*). This would represent a north Israelite vocalization (with contracted diphthong). The Judahite form should probably be vocalized **-aw*, as in Lachish 3.18 *'nšw* (**'anašaw*). The *yod* of the Massoretic form *-āyw* is not to be understood as historical. It is never written in pre-exilic epigraphic Hebrew. Massoretic *-āyw* is a mixed form, with pronunciation *-aw* reflecting Judahite usage (see Hexaplaric *-aw*), and the written *yod* a *mater* suggesting northern *-ê*. See the discussion of Cross and Freedman, *Early Hebrew Orthography* (AOS 36; New Haven: American Oriental Society, 1952) 54-55, 68-69. On Gezer *yrḥw*, see also Albright, "The Gezer Calendar," *BASOR* 92 (1943) 16-26, especially 22, and the discussion of Donner and Röllig in *KAI* 2:181-82.

[7] "Graffiti," 28-30.

[8] Lemaire, "Les inscriptions," 602, and "Yahweh's Asherah?" 44. P.D. Miller ("Psalms and Inscriptions," *Congress Volume, Vienna 1980* [VTSup 32; Leiden: Brill, 1981] 317) translates "Blessed is Uriyahu by Yahweh; Yea from his adversaries

tion is nonetheless very speculative, and few have followed him. Both Zevit and Lemaire read *l'šrth* in line five as well, lending credence to the reading in line three. It may also occur in line six.[9]

If the word asherah occurs in this inscription, what is its meaning? Since the context is so obscure, this is impossible to determine with any certainty. Lemaire read "his asherah" here, arguing that the cult symbol is intended. Zevit has argued that scholars should cease viewing the *he* as a pronominal suffix, and instead read an otherwise unattested form of the goddess's name, **'ašērātâ*. This proposed form would be doubly marked as a feminine noun.[10] Although such a form is not linguistically impossible, it is nonetheless unattested, and in a relatively common word/name in Biblical Hebrew and other Canaanite dialects. This cautions against the acceptance of Zevit's suggestion. A. Angerstorfer has also argued that the word be vocalized as a proper noun, and he too proposes an unattested form *'ašîrtâ*, based on the evidence of variant Bronze Age forms of the goddess name. But none of these variant forms supports any suggestion for double marking, though one could argue for a stem *'ašîrt-* based on them.[11] Amarna/ Ugaritic *'aš/ṭirt-/'aš/ṭart-* would be **'ašeret* in Biblical Hebrew and *'aširt* or *'ašart* in epigraphic Hebrew. Amarna/ Akkadian/ Ugaritic *'aš/ṭrat-* would be *'ašrâ* in Biblical Hebrew or epigraphic Hebrew.[12] Thus, both of the proposed doubly marked feminine name forms are unlikely. We tend to agree with Lemaire's understanding of el-Qôm *'šrth* as the common noun asherah with suffix "his," but little more can be said about this inscription because of its various difficulties. In light of this, we shall proceed to the evidence from Kuntillet Ajrûd, about which much more can be said with confidence.

Articles began to appear in the journals in the late 1970's seeking to interpret the data from Kuntillet Ajrûd. An intriguing inscription *brkt 'tkm lyhwh šmrn wl'šrth* appears on a pithos covered with a variety of rather crude drawings. Variations on this blessing were discovered on other pithoi, which in-

---

by his asherah he has saved him." This translation requires no emendation of the text, and is followed by Day, "Asherah," 395 n.34.

[9] For line six, Lemaire reads only *ŕ ḥ*, where Zevit reads . . .'*ʔʔrth*.

[10] "Khirbet el-Qôm," 45-46. He compares **'ašērātâ* to names like *'eprātâ, yotbātâ*, and *timnātâ*.

[11] "Asherah als 'consort of Jahwe,'" 7-16, see especially 11 ff. "Daher möchte ich einen *Gottesnamen* '*Ašîrtāh* lesen, bei dem /h/ nicht Suffix, sondern Schreibung der femininen Formen auf -*āh* darstellt."

[12] De Moore ("'*ăshērāh*," 438) discusses this.

clude the words *lyhwh tmn wl'šrth*. Scholars still await the full publication of this material,[13] though many of the drawings have been published recently in *Tel Aviv*.[14] Z. Meshel, the archeologist who undertook the excavation, has published a number of papers on the subject.[15] Originally, he argued that *šmrn* was to be understood as **šōmirinū*, "our guardian," and *'šrth* as "his sanctuary." Thus, to paraphrase Meshel, "I bless you by Yahweh our guardian and his sanctuary." Meshel's most recent published opinion is found in *Biblical Archaeology Review* (1979), where he argues that "his cella," "his tree symbol" or "his consort" (proposing this unattested meaning for the noun asherah) are all possible readings in this context.[16] By 1979, Meshel was reading *šmrn* as **šōmirōn*, "Samaria," along with most scholars who have studied the evidence.[17] He stated that the goddess Asherah may have been Yahweh's consort in some circles.

In 1978/79, M. Gilula published a stimulating treatment on the subject of the inscriptions and the drawings on pithos A.[18] He points out that asherah never means sanctuary in Hebrew, unlike in Akkadian and Phoenician. The word in Hebrew always denotes the goddess or her cult symbol.[19] He argues that Asherah is Yahweh's consort here: the two front figures are

[13] The *editio princeps* has not yet appeared. For the time being, see Z. Meshel, "Consort," 24-36, where a number of photographs appear.

[14] Beck, "The Drawings," 3-86.

[15] "Kuntilat ʿAjrûd—An Israelite Site from the Monarchical Period on the Sinai Border," *Qadmoniot* 9 (1976) 118-24 (Hebrew); "Kuntillet ʿAjrûd—An Israelite Religious Center in the Northern Sinai," *Expedition* 20 (1978) 50-54; *Kuntillet ʿAjrûd: A Religious Centre from the Time of the Judaean Monarchy* (Museum Catalogue 175; Jerusalem: Israel Museum, 1978); "Consort," 24-36.

[16] "If Asherah had the generic meaning of a female deity who was Yahweh's consort, then the possessive form could have been used" ("Consort" 31). But there is no evidence anywhere that it ever had such a meaning. See Lemaire, "Les inscriptions," 603-608, for a review of the possible meanings of Hebrew asherah. Emerton, ("New Light," 15) also opposes this. The term asherah is attested in Akkadian and Phoenician with the meaning sanctuary. See *AHw* 1.80 for Akkadian examples, and *KAI* 19.4, the Maʿṣûb inscription, a dedication to Aštart in the sanctuary (*b'šrt*) of Baal Ḥamon. A recently published ostracon from Akko mentions a Baal-shaalti, "who is in charge of the asherah" (*'š 'l 'šrt*). See provisionally M. Dothan, "The Phoenician Inscription from ʿAkko," *Eretz Israel* 18 (1985) 116-23 (Hebrew) and "A Phoenician Inscription from ʿAkko," *IEJ* 35 (1985) 81-94 and pl. 13A and B. On the idiom *'š 'l*, see Dothan, *IEJ* 35:85-86. I should like to thank P. Kyle McCarter, Jr., for bringing this inscription to my attention, and for providing me with his reading.

[17] "Consort," 31.

[18] "To Yahweh Shomron," 129-37.

[19] E. Lipiński has argued that the word asherah in the Hebrew Bible should be understood in virtually all cases as "sanctuary" or "cella." In Judges 6 and Deut 16:21, it should be taken as "sacred grove." He states that "it seems that no biblical

Yahweh and Asherah standing together. The penis or tail of the right hand figure is a later addition; we can tell it is female by its breasts. The figure on the left has bovine features, and Gilula suggests that here Yahweh is portrayed in the form of a bull, consistent with the iconographic traditions of the northern kingdom. Gilula does not account for the third figure on the far right, a female (?) who is playing a musical instrument and sitting on a chair or throne. He admits that there is no certainty that the inscription was intended to describe the drawing. The reading of the inscription which Gilula offers is "to Yahweh of Samaria and his asherah," with "his asherah" understood as the cult symbol representing the goddess.[20]

In 1979, J. Naveh discussed the inscription briefly in his article "Graffiti and Dedications."[21] He argues for the reading "Yahweh our guardian," against "Yahweh of Samaria," based on the observation that Phoenician-style defective spelling is evident at the end of words in the Ajrûd corpus.[22] This, however, is true only in certain cases (*yhw* of the stone bowl, *brkt* of the inscription under consideration). The divine name is spelled *plene* in the inscription we are discussing and elsewhere in the corpus (*yhwh tmn*, pithos B). Thus, there is some orthographic inconsistency in the Ajrûd inscriptions, so that Naveh's argument for reading "our guardian" (*šōmirinū*) is not particularly compelling.

J. Emerton's 1982 article on these inscriptions stands as one of the best treatments to date.[23] Emerton points out that the reading *yhwh tmn* (*têman*) in other Ajrûd inscriptions supports Gilula's suggestion that *šmrn* here is to be read "Samaria."[24]

passage mentions the goddess Atirat or her emblem" ("The Goddess Atirat," 101-19). See the thorough critique of Emerton, "New Light," 15-18.

[20] "To Yahweh Shomron," 134. McCarter agrees with Gilula on most points ("Religion of the Israelite Monarchy" 146-47). Against this position, see Stolz, "Monotheismus in Israel," 168-70.

[21] 27-30.

[22] For example, *brkt* instead of *brkty* in the blessing on pithos A, and *yhw* (*yahwē*) on the stone bowl, but see *yhwh* on pithos A and pithos B, '*srth*, with -*h* marking the suffix, and so on. Defective orthography appears inconsistently in the Kuntillet Ajrûd corpus.

[23] "New Light," 1-20.

[24] Ibid., 9-10. It is unlikely that Teman is the name of a particular town. Rather, it appears to be a geographical term which refers to a region of Edom, and perhaps also a term used for Edom in toto. Hab 3:3 suggests this: '*ĕlôah mittêmān yābô*' // *wĕqādôš mēhar-pā'rān*. Elsewhere, Paran is used, as is Seir, for the region of Edom (Deut 33:2 Seir // Paran; Judg 5:4 Seir // Edom). See R. de Vaux, "Téman, ville ou région d'Édom?" *RB* 76 (1969) 379-85. In Gen 36:11, Teman appears in an Edomite genealogy. McCarter ("Religion of the Israelite Monarchy") presents a

Emerton feels that it is unlikely that a cult of Yahweh ever existed in the Teman region. Rather, this is probably a general statement about Yahweh's associations with the Edomite southland (see Hab 3:3).[25] We doubt that Emerton is correct on this point. Yahweh's close associations with the deep south in early texts suggests at least that his cult was present there, perhaps even prominent. Emerton argues that 'šrth is best taken as a reference to the cult symbol and not the personal name of the goddess: "This understanding of the word fits the inscriptions from Kuntillet Ajrud. People are blessed by Yahweh and the wooden symbol of the goddess Asherah."[26] He notes that there is no evidence for Meshel's "generic sense" of asherah; in the Hebrew Bible, the word refers either to the deity or to her symbol. Since there is as yet no evidence in Biblical or epigraphic Hebrew that a pronominal suffix is ever attached to a proper noun, 'šrth in the inscription should be taken to refer to the cult symbol.[27] Against the "sanctuary" understanding suggested by Meshel for these inscriptions (and argued in depth by E. Lipiński for all but two occurrences of asherah in the Hebrew Bible), Emerton argues that this meaning of the noun is improbable in Hebrew. All of Lipiński's examples can be better explained by the traditional theory that the asherah is a cult symbol of the goddess of that name.[28] Emerton concludes: "The Asherah invoked in the phrase 'Yahweh and his Asherah' is probably the wooden symbol of the goddess of that name, whose association with the cult of Yahweh is attested in the Old Testament. She may have been regarded in some circles as the consort of Yahweh, but the inscriptions do not offer direct proof of such a relationship."[29] Emerton is overly cautious in his final evalua-

---

penetrating discussion of the local cults of Yahweh, as well as a treatment of the form DN of GN in Northwest Semitic.

[25] "New Light," 3.

[26] Ibid., 15. Followed by Day, "Asherah," 391.

[27] Ibid., 14. This observation, as Emerton notes, is not altered by G. R. Driver's list of such usages in other Semitic languages ("Reflections on Recent Articles," *JBL* 73 [1954] 125, in his discussion of the name Yahweh). Others have discussed the pronominal suffix problem in the Kuntillet Ajrûd inscriptions. See Zevit, "Goddess," 45, and for Khirbet el-Qôm 3, Lemaire, "Les inscriptions," 607 ("En effet, la forme grammaticale 'šrth nous confirme que 'šrh était un nom commun puisqu'il est suivi du suffixe personnel: il s'agit donc probablement d'un objet et non d'une divinité quelconque 'Ashérah' ").

[28] Emerton, ibid., 16-18. On Lipiński, see note 19. Lipiński suggested emendation in the case of Judg 3:7 (*hā' ǎšērôt* > *hā'aštārôt* with Baal, as in Judg 2:13; 10:6; 1 Sam 7:4; 12:10), and 1 Kgs 18:19. He is certainly correct to regard 1 Kgs 18:19 as a gloss.

[29] Emerton, ibid., 19. Day, "Asherah," 392 believes the inscription suggests Ashe-

tion of the implications of the inscriptions for our understanding of both popular and state Yahwism in the monarchic period. They suggest strongly that Asherah was Yahweh's consort in state religion as well as popular religion in the northern kingdom.

P. Beck published the drawings from Kuntillet Ajrûd in 1982.[30] Included in her study is a detailed commentary on possible Near Eastern sources of influence on the style employed by the artists responsible for the Ajrûd drawings.[31] Her remarks on the three figures below the inscription mentioning Yahweh šōmĕrôn and his asherah are instructive. Gilula had argued that the two foreground figures were Yahweh and Asherah. Beck, on the other hand, states that "there is no doubt that they represent the god Bes, a collective name for a group of Egyptian dwarf deities."[32] Her arguments on this point are convincing. She also suggests that the two Bes figures are probably not by the same artist,[33] and doubts whether there is any direct relationship between the inscription and the drawings.[34] Beck cautions that we ought not to reach hasty conclusions even about the sex of the lyre player. There is no certainty that it is a woman: "The nipples do not necessarily identify the lyre player as female. On the Hubbard amphora from Cyprus. . .nipples appear on men and women alike, the transparent garment through which they are visible being worn by both sexes. It would seem therefore that the lyre player could be defined as a woman only on the strength of her hairdo and skirt."[35] Beck argues that the Bes figure on the right foreground was drawn by the same artist who drew the lyre player.[36] She does not attempt to identify the musician, but does relate the style employed in the drawing of the three figures to the "desert art" of

rah was Yahweh's consort in a "syncretistic" cult. He also cites Deut 16:21-22. According to Day, these beliefs reflect a form of "popular religion."

[30] See note 3.

[31] See Dever's criticisms of Beck's approach in "Asherah," 31-32, n.4 which are overstated. The art-historical approach of Beck is a welcome contribution to the discussion, and should be taken seriously by biblical scholars and epigraphers who are considering the possible relationship between the drawings and the inscription.

[32] Beck, "The Drawings," 29. See also the remarks of Stolz, "Monotheismus in Israel," 168, who argues the figures are Bes. On Bes, see W. Helck and E. Otto, *Lexikon der Ägyptologie* (Wiesbaden: Harrassowitz, 1975) 1.719-21.

[33] Ibid. 31.

[34] Ibid. 45-47. The three figures were painted with a thick brush. The inscription was written with a thinner brush. Beck argues that the inscription was added after both Bes figures had been drawn.

[35] Ibid. 31.

[36] Ibid. 36.

Arabia and the Negeb.[37] Beck's remarks about the tree-ibex-lion scene on pithos A are worth noting in passing. She doubts whether this is related to any particular deity.[38] We shall have more to say about this.

W. Dever recently published his views on the inscriptions and drawings. "I shall attempt to show that 'Yahweh's asherah' at 'Ajrûd (and possibly at el-Qôm) may refer to the goddess herself—that is, to Asherah as a hypostatization of the Great Goddess, not simply to the use of the word 'asherah' to refer to an attribute or cult-image."[39] Dever argues that the lyre player (whom he takes to be female)[40] provides the key for the interpretation of both the inscription and the scene below it. The two figures in the foreground are representations of the god Bes, as Beck argued (this against Gilula), but the lyre player is an enthroned goddess, Asherah herself. The mention of Asherah and her appearance in the drawing "strongly suggest that she was revered as the consort of Yahweh in some circles in ancient Israel."[41] Dever notes the issue of the pronominal suffix, but does not deal with it in any depth.[42]

Beck's arguments about the relationship of the drawings to the inscriptions must be considered seriously. Neither the arguments of Gilula nor those of Dever relating the drawings to the inscription on pithos A are especially convincing. In each case, significant questions remain unanswered. If, as Gilula argued, Yahweh and Asherah are the two foreground figures, who then is the lyre player and why is she not mentioned in the inscription? One would expect that all three figures would be mentioned if the inscription does describe the drawings. How can it be proved that the penis/tail of the right foreground figure is secondary? Why are Yahweh and Asherah portrayed as Bes figures? These unanswered questions and Beck's observations concerning the relationship of all three figures suggest that the drawings and inscription have only an accidental relationship of proximity.

Similar questions are raised by Dever's thesis. If Asherah is the lyre player, why are the two Bes figures present in the fore-

---

[37] Ibid. 36.

[38] Ibid. 16. This is far less doubtful than Beck suggests. The tree is probably an asherah.

[39] Dever, "Asherah," 22.

[40] Though Beck argues that this is questionable, most scholars would agree that the musician is a woman.

[41] Dever, "Asherah," 30.

[42] Ibid. 30.

ground? They seem to be the focus of the drawing, yet they are not mentioned in the inscription. There is a less problematic explanation for the presence of the lyre player. The musician is easily explained by the presence of the Bes figures. Bes in Egyptian religion danced and had prominent musical associations. We suggest that the background figure here is simply a musician playing for the dancing Bes figures in the foreground. Asherah, in extant literary texts, is never associated with music, though Tannit of the Punic west is sometimes portrayed with tambourine. There are other problems. The cult symbol interpretation suggested by Emerton for this inscription and by Lemaire for el-Qôm 3 is certainly the most convincing, as they have shown. Dever has not considered the suffix problem sufficiently. "His asherah" suggests strongly that the goddess's proper name is excluded unless we are to argue for a hitherto unattested use of a pronominal suffix on a proper noun in Hebrew. The cult object interpretation does not raise this difficulty, or any other for that matter.

Dever asks, "Is it logical to suppose that an inanimate object, or even a sanctuary, could be mentioned on an equal footing with the principal deity as an agent of blessing, as the context demands both at ʿAjrûd and at el-Qôm?" It certainly is! The cult symbol represents the goddess, and the close association of symbol and deity in Near Eastern religion has been much discussed.[43] Let us take for example the case of bull iconography. The creature could function as a throne of deity, as in the case of Yahweh at Dan and Bethel, and in numerous reliefs depicting the storm god standing on the back of a bull.[44] At the same time, the bull could function as a symbol of the deity himself, as in the Hittite relief from Alaʿa Hüyük, which depicts a king and queen (?) before an altar, behind which a bull representing the storm god stands on a raised pedestal.[45] There are other repre-

---

[43] See the recent discussion of A. Mazar regarding bull iconographic traditions in the Ancient Near East ("The 'Bull Site'—An Iron Age I Open Cult Place," *BASOR* 247 [1982] 27-42).

[44] On the bulls as pedestals for Yahweh, see Albright, *From Stone Age to Christianity* (Garden City: Doubleday/Anchor, 1957) 299-300; Eißfeldt, "Lade und Stierbild," *ZAW* 58 (1940/41) 190-215; Cross, *Canaanite Myth* 73; de Vaux, *Ancient Israel* 333. The storm god is depicted on the back of a bull in various reliefs, including those from Carchemish, Arslan Tash, and Barsip. See *ANEP* 500, 501, and 531, as well as 537, the Assyrian Maltaya relief, which portrays a procession of gods standing on animal thrones. Adad is the sixth figure from the left.

[45] *ANEP* 616. The bull's genitalia are prominent, as they are in the case of the recently discovered bronze bull from the Iron I site near Mt. Gilboa (see Mazar, "The 'Bull Site,' " 27-42). This suggests strength and fertility.

sentations which depict the storm god holding a reined bull.[46] Here, the bull functions as the sacred animal of the god, reflecting attributes commonly associated with him (strength, fertility). The bull in the West Semitic world could be associated with either Baal-Haddu, El or, in Israel, Yahweh. The deity and his or her symbol are inseparable.[47] This could lead to some confusion between god and symbol, as occurred in the case of the bull icons of the northern sanctuaries. Hosea's condemnations of the bull icon of Bethel should be seen in this light.[48] In the inscriptions from Kuntillet Ajrûd, the asherah, as a symbol of the goddess Asherah, is named alongside Yahweh in a blessing. This should not occasion surprise, since naming the cult symbol of the deity is synonymous with naming the deity herself.

The reading *šōmirōn has been accepted by a majority of scholars who have commented on the inscriptions, including Meshel, Gilula, Emerton, and Dever and Lemaire. Naveh preferred the reading *šōmirinū, "our guardian," which was Meshel's original suggestion. This interpretation was also accepted by Angerstorfer. But as Emerton has shown, the parallel expression yhwh tmn, "Yahweh, the one of Teman," suggests that Samaria is meant by šmrn in yhwh šmrn.[49] But there is more evidence in favor of reading "Samaria." A paleographic analysis indicates that the inscription is of northern provenance and that it is to be dated to ca. 800. The writing is remarkably similar to that of the earlier Samaria Ostraca (ca. 775), perhaps a generation older.[50] We know from the Hebrew Bible that Ahab (ca. 875-54) erected an asherah in Samaria (1 Kgs 16:33) and that it remained standing there long after Jehu's conservative Yahwistic reform (ca. 841), down to the end of the ninth century

---

[46] See the MB seals from Alalakh in D. Collon, *The Seal Impressions from Tell Atchana/Alalakh* (AOAT 27; Neukirchen-Vluyn: Neukirchener/ Kevelaer: Butzon & Bercker, 1975) 8: 25, 34, 41. For a similar LB motif, see W.F. Petrie, *Ancient Gaza V* (London: British School of Egyptian Archaeology, 1952) 9: 33.

[47] See Cross, *Canaanite Myth* 73.

[48] Hos 8:5-6; 10:5-6; 13:2. In 8:6 Hosea emphasizes that the icon is not a god *per se: wĕhû' ḥārāš 'āśāhû// wĕlō' 'ĕlōhîm hû'* ("As for him, a craftsman made him// He is no god!").

[49] See most recently Lemaire, "Date et origine," 132, who accepts the "Samaria" reading.

[50] On the writing of the Samaria Ostraca, see I.T. Kaufman, "The Samaria Ostraca: An Early Witness to Hebrew Writing," *BA* 45.4 (1982) 229-39. Weinfeld ("Kuntillet 'Ajrud," 131) notes that the forthcoming pottery analysis confirms the date of ca. 800 for the Kuntillet Ajrûd blessings. McCarter ("Religion of the Israelite Monarchy," 138) assigns a date of ca. 790 to the inscriptions on the basis of paleography, text analysis and historical considerations. He notes that Israel controlled Judah at that time (see 2 Kgs 14:7-16).

(2 Kgs 13:6).[51] This must be the same asherah mentioned in the blessings from Ajrûd. When the biblical and epigraphic data are correlated, the chronology certainly fits. Additional evidence for the northern provenance of these inscriptions is found in their onomasticon. Names with the *-yaw (-yw) theophoric element are common, an indicator of northern origin. In this period, the form *-yahû (-yhw) predominated in Judah.[52] These data, when considered en masse, are convincing evidence for the reading "Yahweh, the one of Samaria."

What of the pronominal suffix -h in 'šrth? It could represent either the 3 ms or the 3 fs in this period.[53] Thus, we could read *'aširatuh, "his asherah," or *'aširatāh, "its asherah," referring to Samaria.[54] Since we know of the famous asherah of Samaria from biblical sources, the latter reading is appealing. Yet it is not significant whether one reads "his" or "its" here. What is important is the mention of the asherah in connection with the cult of Yahweh. Zevit's suggestion that we read the -h not as a suffix but as a part of a hitherto unattested form of the goddess's name both in el-Qôm and Ajrûd has little to commend it.[55]

The biblical evidence examined in Chapter 1 suggests that the asherah was a cult symbol representing the goddess Asherah, which was an acceptable and legitimate part of Yahweh's cult in non-deuteronomistic circles. This association of the asherah and the cult of Yahweh suggests in turn that Asherah was the consort of Yahweh in circles both in the north and the south.

---

[51] The text of 2 Kgs 13:6 says it remained at Jehoahaz's death, circa 798. On the debate concerning the date of Jehu's coup, see recently B. Halpern, "Yaua, Son of Omri, Yet Again," *BASOR* 265 (1987) 81-85.

[52] See pithos A PN yw'šh (*yaw'ašā) and pithos B 'mryw (*'amaryaw) comparing Samaria Ostraca PNs in -yw. The two stone bowls from Kuntillet Ajrûd have 'bdyw (*'abdyaw) and šm'yw (*šama'yaw). In Khirbet el-Qôm 3, the PN 'ryhw (*'ūrīyahû) occurs, with Judahite -yhw as expected. The Shemaiah seal, to be dated probably to circa 800, has the PNs šm'yhw and 'zryhw. See D. Diringer, *Le iscrizioni antico-ebraiche palestinesi* (Firenze: Monnier, 1934) 199-200; Pl. xx #10, and Cross and Freedman, *Early Hebrew Orthography* 47-48. On Israelite personal names, and particularly the spelling of the theophoric elements, see R. Lawton, "Israelite Personal Names on Pre-Exilic Hebrew Inscriptions," *Bib* 65 (1984) 330-46, and Tigay, *No Other Gods* 47-89.

[53]

BH	*PH	*PS	
-ōh/-ô	< -uh	< -uhu	(3 m s)
-āh	< -āh	< -aha	(3 f s)

In the Hebrew Bible, the -h form of the 3ms suffix is vestigial, with -w the common, generally levelled orthographic form.

[54] According to McCarter, "Religion of the Israelite Monarchy," 154 n.54, and Tigay, *No Other Gods* 26 n.31, B. Levine suggested this orally as far back as 1980.

[55] "Khirbet el-Qôm," 39-47.

The epigraphic evidence we have examined buttresses this thesis, even if we interpret '*šrth* of the inscriptions as the cult symbol with pronominal suffix and not as the personal name of the goddess, and even if we do not accept arguments that attempt to relate the drawings of Ajrûd pithos A to the inscription above them. The cult symbol represents the goddess, and the cult symbol is clearly tied to Yahweh. It is important to note that we are not speaking only of popular religion here; the asherahs of Samaria, Bethel and Jerusalem were a constituent part of state Yahwism.

Many scholars have suspected that a sanctuary dedicated to Yahweh existed in Samaria, though it is never mentioned in the biblical text. Hosea 8:5, *zānaḥ ʿeglēk šōmĕrôn* ("He has spurned your calf, Samaria") suggests this, if we are to take *šōmĕrôn* as the city and not as a term for the northern kingdom.[56] The meaning of *šōmĕrôn* here, however, remains uncertain. An opposing view, that Samaria was the exclusively "Canaanite" cult and political center of the northern kingdom, was presented by A. Alt and has been defended in recent years by H. Donner.[57] According to this thesis, the Omrides put into practice a politico-religious dualism, separating the "Israelite" and "Canaanite" elements in their state. The Yahwistic cult centers were Dan and Bethel, and Jezreel served as the capital for the "Israelite" segment of the population, while Samaria, an autonomous city-state, was the focus of "Canaanite" cult and government.[58]

[56] Generally, scholars agree that "Samaria" is used of the northern kingdom only after the Assyrian conquest. However, there may be some exceptions to this pattern. Wolff (*Hosea* 140) argues that the city Samaria is meant in Hos 8:5. Against him, Rudolph (*Hosea* 164) argues that Bethel is meant. See also Nowack (*Die kleinen Propheten* 51) who believes that "Samaria" does not necessarily mean the city in all Hosea passages. In Hos 7:1 and 14:1, "Samaria" seems to have a regional meaning. Also, Adad-Nirari III uses "Samaria" to describe the country ([KUR]*Sa-me-ri-na-a-a*). See S. Timm (*Dynastie Omri* 151) for discussion. Many would emend Massoretic *zānaḥ* of 8:5 to **zānaḥtî* based on the first person subject of the next colon.

[57] Alt, "Der Stadtstaat Samaria," in *Kleine Schriften* 3:258-302; "The Monarchy in the Kingdom of Israel and Judah," in *Essays on Old Testament History and Religion*, tr. R.A. Wilson (Oxford: Blackwell, 1966) 241-59; Donner, *Herrschergestalten in Israel* (Verständliche Wissenschaft 103; Berlin, Heidelberg and New York: Springer, 1970) 58-71; "The Separate States of Israel and Judah," in *Israelite and Judaean History*, ed. J.H. Hayes and J.M. Miller (Old Testament Library; Philadelphia: Westminster, 1977) 401. J. Gray (*I & II Kings* [2nd ed.; Old Testament Library; London: SCM, 1970] 366-67) accepts the solution proposed by these scholars.

[58] A comprehensive critique of this hypothesis is found in S. Timm, *Dynastie Omri* 142-48. Equally worth noting is the review of Alt's essay/monograph by de Vaux, *RB* 63 (1956) 100-106. There are many speculative aspects to Alt's reconstruction.

The inscriptions mentioning Yahweh *šōmĕrôn* now make it clear that a Yahwistic sanctuary existed in Samaria, and that the asherah stood in it.[59] Clearly, arguments for political and religious dualism in the north under the Omrides can no longer be sustained. Samaria was the capital of the kingdom, with a sanctuary dedicated to Yahweh and also the temple dedicated to Baal mentioned in the texts of Kings. This is certainly not a surprise. The capital of a state ought to have a sanctuary dedicated to the national god, in this case Yahweh. The exact status of the Baal temple remains unclear.

A dearth of onomastic evidence for Asherah's worship in Israel is evident both in the Hebrew Bible and in the Israelite epigraphic corpus.[60] Assuming Asherah was the consort of Yahweh according to the beliefs of some or many Israelites, should we not then expect at least some personal names to be extant with Asherah as theophoric element? The problem is really not so simple, as a survey of the comparative onomastic and epigraphic evidence shows. In general, there is no direct correlation between the importance of the deities of the official cult (myths, pantheon lists and royal inscriptions) and the gods of popular piety, as reflected in personal names and dedications. In recent discussions of this problem, D. Pardee[61] and J. Tigay[62]

The possibility of Israelite non-*naḥălâ* ownership is readily admitted by Alt himself ("Stadtstaat," 265 n.1). Shemer could have been a Yahwist selling Omri non-patrimonial property. There is no evidence that Samaria was ever a "city-state" within the Israelite kingdom as such. The exchange of letters between Jehu and the elders in 2 Kings 10 should be viewed as a literary device meant to build suspense, and not as evidence of Samaria's political independence from the rest of Israel. See the criticisms of G. Buccellati, *Cities and Nations of Ancient Syria* (Studi Semitici 26; Rome: University of Rome, 1967) 190, and Timm, ibid., 146, who argues that Jehu simply wanted the officials of Samaria to do the dirty work for him. Jehu's call for an Omride rival must be interpreted in light of the traditions of popular kingship in the north, and not as an indicator of Samaria's separate status. See, for example, the civil war between Omri, Zimri and Tibni, where different groups acclaimed rival candidates who fought it out until Omri emerged in control of the throne. Timm notes that the Yahwist Jehu ruled in Samaria and was buried there (147). This seems unusual if Samaria were really an exclusively Canaanite capital and cult center. There are obviously many reasons to oppose the hypothesis of Alt and Donner. There are more convincing ways to explain the evolution of the society and the political system of the north.

[59] Timm examined the biblical data suggesting a sanctuary of Yahweh in Samaria and concluded that the evidence was ambiguous (ibid., 148-56). Yet he leans toward a positive evaluation.

[60] I should like to take this opportunity to thank Gary A. Anderson for pointing this problem out to me, and to thank both Gary A. Anderson and Ronald S. Hendel for their suggestions in this regard.

[61] "An Evaluation of the Proper Names from Ebla from a West Semitic Perspec-

reach this conclusion. After observing the scarcity of non-Yahweh/El names in the Hebrew epigraphic onomasticon, Tigay notes the remarkable absence of goddess names (none with Asherah, Anat or Aštart; one with Isis; one with '*dt*).[63] Tigay notes a similar situation with the onomasticon of Ammon, where only El/Milkom appear as theophoric elements in names.[64] At Ugarit, not one Aštart theophoric name occurs, and only one with Asherah,[65] though these goddesses play relatively important secondary roles in the myths, receive sacrifices in lists of offerings, and are listed in pantheon tabulations.[66] Tigay concludes that by the fourteenth/thirteenth centuries at Ugarit, the goddesses played a minor role in popular religion though they remained important in the official cultus.[67] Tigay's points are well taken, though the relationship between popular piety and official religion is more complex than he assumes, and his conclusion that the goddesses have lost their popular appeal does not necessarily follow, as we shall see.

Evidence from New Kingdom Egypt differs little from the Ugaritic data. Though Aštart plays a significant role in the official cult,[68] very few personal names formed with Aštart are extant.[69] In the Punic west of the mid- to late first millennium,

---

tive: Pantheon Distribution According to Genre," forthcoming in the proceedings of the conference "The Onomasticon of Ebla: Semitic Name-Giving and Eblaic Prosopography," Rome, 15-17 Luglio, 1985. Professor Pardee was kind enough to allow me to read the manuscript before publication.

[62] *No Other Gods* 18-20, especially 20.

[63] Ibid. 13-14.

[64] Ibid. 19 and n.60. Tigay recognizes Milkom as an El epithet. See K.P. Jackson, *The Ammonite Language of the Iron Age* (HSM 27; Chico, CA.: Scholars, 1983) 95-98 for an onomastic list.

[65] Tigay, *No Other Gods* 20. Twelve names occur for Anat. See Grøndahl, *Die Personennamen der Texte aus Ugarit* (Studia Pohl 1; Rome: Pontifical Biblical Institute, 1967) 83 for Anat; 103 for Asherah.

[66] Tigay, *No Other Gods* 20.

[67] Ibid. 20. See Tigay's n.64 for a fine bibliography on the relation of official and popular religion.

[68] On this see R. Stadelmann, *Syrisch-Palästinensische Gottheiten in Ägypten* (Probleme der Ägyptologie 5; Leiden: Brill, 1967) 96-110; J. Leclant, "Astarté à cheval d'après les représentations égyptiennes," *Syria* 37 (1960) 1-67; W. Herrmann, "Aštart," *Mitteilungen des Instituts für Orientforschung* 15 (1969) 6-55; Olyan, "Some Observations Concerning the Identity of the Queen of Heaven," *UF* 19 (1988) forthcoming.

[69] Herrmann, ibid., 39 claims none are attested, but two are listed by W. Helck, *Die Beziehungen Ägyptens zu Vorderasien im 3. und 2. Jahrtausend v. Chr.* (Ägyptologische Abhandlungen 5; Wiesbaden: Harrassowitz, 1962) 492, and two others are listed by H. Ranke, *Ägyptischen Personennamen* (Glückstadt: J.J. Augustin, 1977) 3.36.

thousands of stelae dedicated to Tannit have been unearthed, yet personal names formed with Tannit are few in number.[70] In contrast, hundreds of Aštart names are extant, while Aštart plays a relatively minor role in the dedicatory inscriptions. This is most striking.

There are no convincing explanations for this unusual pattern in piety which we have observed in Israel, at Ugarit, in New Kingdom Egypt and in the Punic sphere. In a number of cases, the major goddesses of the official cult rarely (if ever) appear in personal names. Aštart in the Punic world is the major exception. In several cases (Israel, Ugarit, and perhaps the Punic west), the evidence pertains to Asherah. Tigay's explanation for this pattern at Ugarit (the evidence suggests that the goddesses play a minor role in popular religion though they remain important in the official cult) will not work either for Israel or for the Punic west. The Kuntillet Ajrûd and Khirbet el-Qôm inscriptions are certainly expressions of popular piety rather than pronouncements of the official cultus. The thousands of Tannit dedications from the Punic world are likewise attestations of popular religion. What we observe in Israel and the Punic west are two contrasting corpora of evidence for popular belief (names on the one hand and dedications/blessings on the other). No theory about the nature or role of the goddesses explains this evidence because it is so inconsistent. As a result of our examination of the comparative onomastic data, it should be clear that a lack of personal names compounded with Asherah in Israelite inscriptions or the Bible tells us little about the importance of the goddess in the popular cult, since names are only one source of evidence, and nothing about Asherah's role in official Israelite religion. The Kuntillet Ajrûd and Khirbet el-Qôm data suggest Asherah played some role in Israelite popular religion. The biblical evidence and the Kuntillet Ajrûd inscriptions (by mentioning Yahweh *šōměrôn* and his/its asherah) suggest Asherah had a role in the official cult as well. Just how important Asherah and her symbol were in monarchic Israel is difficult to gauge precisely due to the limitations of the evidence, but the law in Deut 16:21 suggests that her role may have been significant.[71]

---

[70] See n.98, chapter 3. At most, ten individuals each bore one of four Tannit names.

[71] One wonders what was expected of the goddesses by the worshipers naming their children. Perhaps very little in many cases. See Tigay, *No Other Gods* 6.

Chapter 3

YAHWEH AND ASHERAH OR BAAL AND ASHERAH?
THE EVIDENCE FROM CANAANITE RELIGION

It is almost a commonplace in biblical scholarship to assume that Asherah was the consort of Baal in the Iron Age, although she was El's consort in the Bronze Age.[1] The Hebrew Bible is often cited in this regard. This view is usually expressed in passing, often with little or no argumentation, suggesting that few scholars would question it. We intend to call this hypothesis into question, based both on the results of our previous investigation and on an examination of the pertinent evidence from the sources of Canaanite religion in the Late Bronze Age and the Iron Age. We have argued that Asherah was the consort of Yahweh in Israelite circles, in state religion as well as popular religion. We have suggested that the passages where Asherah or her symbol are associated with Baal are best understood as examples of deuteronomistic polemic. They are an accurate reflection of the practice and theology of neither Canaanite nor Israelite religion. The absence of the asherah or Asherah in the Elijah-Elisha narratives, the Jehu stories, and the oracles of Amos and Hosea demand a careful reconsideration of this thesis. All of these narratives oppose the worship of Baal in Israel, and in the case of 1 Kings 18 and 2 Kings 9-10, describe the eradication of Baal's cultus, yet never is Asherah or her symbol mentioned.[2] If Asherah were the consort of Baal in the Iron Age, as so many scholars assume, surely her cult would have been opposed by conservative and even radical Yahwists like Elijah, Jehu, Amos or Hosea. The theory that Asherah is Baal's consort in the Hebrew Bible does not address this silence adequately. In light of the intense rivalry between Yahweh and Baal and their respective votaries during the period of the divided monarchy, it is difficult to imagine that they could share the same consort. Yet it is easy to see detractors of Asherah and her cult symbol such as the deuteronomistic school accord to her the

---

[1] See n.16, chapter 1 for citations.
[2] See our comments earlier on 1 Kgs 18:19; Hos 4:12 and 14:9.

stamp of Yahwistic illegitimacy by associating her with Baal and his cultus in a polemical fashion.

The evidence of Canaanite religion in the Late Bronze Age and the Iron Age tends on the whole to support our thesis. Careful analysis of pertinent sources shows that the religion of the Canaanites/Phoenicians was for the most part conservative. Although there is evidence of some fluidity in the associations of certain goddesses with certain gods, the traditional pairings found in the Bronze Age texts remain, even to the end of the first millennium BCE.[3] The phenomenon of hypostatization and its production of new deities does little to contradict this observation. Gods and goddesses may go by different epithets in the Iron Age,[4] but this does not suggest realignment in their consort associations. Asherah remains El's consort from the Ugaritic mythological texts down to the lore of Sanchuniathon. There is little or no convincing evidence that she becomes the consort of Baal in Iron Age Canaanite religion *pace* A. Kapelrud, M. Pope, U. Cassuto and, more recently, U. Oldenburg.[5] Some texts reflect a measure of fluidity of attributes and even epithets between the three major goddesses Asherah, Aštart and Anat, and in some late material, such as Lucian's *De Dea Syria*, the three are fused into a single great goddess, but Atargatis ought to be understood as a fusion-hypostasis of Anat, Aštart and Asherah, combining aspects of all three, not as a replacement for the individual goddesses. Atargatis can be compared to the many double-fusion hypostases of the first millennium.[6] In general,

---

[3] Our tendency to look at Canaanite religion as relatively conservative is not shared by many scholars. Besides the work of M. Pope, see U. Oldenburg, *The Conflict Between El and Ba'al*. R. Oden (*De Syria Dea* 94) has argued that the distinct character of each of the three great goddesses persisted into the common era in Canaanite cults, though some overlap in epithets, attributes and consorts is attested. On the issue of consorts we see the religion as more conservative than does Oden. We shall argue that Asherah remains the consort of El in the Iron Age, Aštart of Baal and Anat of Baal, though Anat's importance seems to decline as Aštart's increases. Thus, we do not agree with Cross and Oden that Anat appears as the consort of El as well as that of Baal in certain texts (*Canaanite Myth* 43; *De Syria Dea* 95). See ahead for further discussion. In an Aramaic text published by A. Dupont-Sommer ("Une stèle araméenne d'un prêtre de Ba'al trouvée en Égypte," *Syria* 33 [1956] 79-87) Anat occurs as consort of Baal. The spelling '*nwt* is, to Dupont-Sommer, odd ("une graphie aberrante"), however, he does point out the similar form in the place name *bêt 'ănôt* in Josh 15:59, and considers this form a dialectal variant. It probably reflects the later Phoenician shift of **a > ō*. Anat's appearance as Baal's consort occasions no surprise.

[4] See ahead for our discussion of Baal Hamon, Baal Ṣimd, Tannit and Derketô.

[5] See n.7.

[6] Oden (*De Syria Dea*) examines Lucian's work and the traditions of the Syrian Goddess contained in it. He argues convincingly that Atargatis represents not only

even by the turn of the millennium, the goddesses and their cults remained distinct throughout most of the Mediterranean world. For the most part, they bear their archaic epithets, and are characterized by their traditional iconography and mythology. Most important, their consorts have not changed. A close look at the traditions of Sanchuniathon demonstrates this.

In this chapter, we shall focus on the thesis that El loses Asherah to Baal, beginning in Late Bronze texts, due to El's alleged impotence and Baal's assumption of kingship over the gods. As M. Pope has argued, "if El, like Kumarbi [of Hittite mythology], was deposed king of the gods, his baffling status in the Ugaritic mythological texts is thereby clarified."[7] Pope cites

a fusion of Anat and Aštart, as previously recognized, but rather a fusion of all three great goddesses. For the text of Lucian, see the translation of Attridge and Oden, eds., *De Dea Syria* (SBLTT 9; Missoula, MT: Scholars, 1976). See also Albright, "The Evolution of the West-Semitic Divinity ʿAn-ʿAnat-ʿAttâ," *AJSL* 41 (1925) 73-101, 283-85. There is some early evidence from Egypt that the three great goddesses could share a single representation. See I.E.S. Edwards, "A Relief of Qudšu-Astarte-Anath in the Winchester College Collection," *JNES* 14 (1955) 49-51. In the Egyptian Winchester plaque, a Hathor-like goddess appears, who is called by the names of all three great goddesses. Cross (*Canaanite Myth* 34) believes the three have been confused here. Since all have fertility associations, this is not difficult to understand. We believe that this is an example of a triple-fusion hypostasis: a new goddess Qudšu-Aštart-Anat produced through the combination of the three, comparable to Atargatis. There are many extant examples of double-fusion hypostases in Canaanite religion, especially in the late first millennium. See our discussion ahead on Tannitʿaštart, ʾAršap-melqart, Melqart-ṣid, Ṣid-tannit and so on. For alternative views of the Winchester Plaque, see Helck, *Betrachtungen zur Großen Göttin und den ihr verbundenen Gottheiten* (Religion und Kultur der alten Mittelmeerwelt in Parallelforschung 2; Munich and Vienna: Oldenbourg, 1971) 217-21. Helck sees Qudšu as an Egyptian "theological speculation," a generic name for the holy female image. R. Stadelmann (*Syrisch-Palästinensische Gottheiten*, 115) translates "Die 'Heiligkeit der Anat' und die 'Heiligkeit der Astarte.'" The triple-fusion hypostasis explanation better accounts for the single image here, and presents no problems for the historian since we see this type of phenomenon elsewhere.

[7] *El in the Ugaritic Texts* (Leiden: Brill, 1955) 32, 35-42. See also A.S. Kapelrud, *Baal in the Ras Shamra Texts* (Copenhagen: Gad, 1952) 64-93, whom Pope follows, as well as the treatments of U. Cassuto, *The Goddess Anath* (English ed.; Jersualem: Magnes, 1971) 55-57, 59, 67, and Oldenburg, *The Conflict Between El and Baʿal* 101-63. These scholars tend on the whole to look for analogues in the mythology of Hesiod (*Theogony*) and the Hurrio-Hittite myths of Kumarbi and Tešub. For the latter material, see H.G. Güterbock, *Kumarbi, Mythen von churritischen Kronos* (New York: Europaverlag, 1946), and "The Song of Ullikummi: Revised Text of the Hittite Version," *JCS* 5 (1951) 135-61; 6 (1951) 8-42. Translations by Goetze are to be found in *ANET* 120-25. The view that El was deposed by Baal is problematic in light of Sanchuniathon's lore, which suggests strongly that this was not the case. Zeus/Demaros/Adados and Astarte rule with the permission of Kronos (*ebasileuon tēs chōras kronou gnōmēi; PE* 1.10.31). See the treatments of Cross, *Canaanite*

El's relationship with Asherah as evidence for this thesis, describing El as "maritally estranged" from Asherah. He discusses the Elkunirsa fragment.[8] In this text, El gives Baal (called "the storm god") permission to sleep with Asherah after she has attempted to seduce Baal. Pope argues that this is a sign of El's impotence or at least his indifference toward Asherah, and concludes from the fact that Asherah sleeps with Baal that Asherah was on the way to becoming Baal's consort even in the Late Bronze Age.[9] Hebrew Bible texts are cited where Baal and Asherah are associated, as well as an offering list from Ugarit where a dedication of an ox (*'alpu) is made "to Baal and Asherah" (lb' l w'aṯrt).[10] Pope also cites a similar dedication "to El and Asherah," noting that in the Late Bronze Age the "transfer" is not yet complete, as indicated by these two dedications.[11] Pope is in agreement with Kapelrud's statement that "the first goddess of the pantheon must be the consort of the first god, and as Baal, apparently slowly, drove out Il from the leading place,

---

Myth 13-43 passim, and T. Mullen, *The Divine Council in Canaanite and Early Hebrew Literature* (HSM 24; Chico, CA: Scholars, 1980) 92-110 with citations, who argue against the views of Pope et al. concerning El and Baal. Mullen notes that El's proclamation of Yamm's lordship does not necessarily suggest El in conflict with Baal (*CTA* 1.4.17; 2.3.7-9). It is El's responsibility as executive of the council to proclaim a ruler of the cosmos. If anything, this shows El's prevailing authority over the gods. In this regard, see *CTA* 6.6.22-31, where Šapaš warns Môt not to fight Baal any longer, or El will overthrow him. Môt desists, reacting with fear. In *CTA* 2.3.15-19, Šapaš warns Aṭtar to obey El. The reaction is similar. On the theme of divine rank and authority, see M.S. Smith, "Divine Travel as a Token of Divine Rank," *UF* 16 (1984) 359. A number of other scholars have opposed the thesis that El is overthrown by Baal. See Eißfeldt, *El im Ugaritischen Pantheon* (Berlin: Akademie, 1951) 60-70; F. Løkkegaard, "Baalsfald," *DTT* 19 (1956) 65-82; "A Plea for El the Bull, and other Ugaritic Miscellanies," *Studia Orientalia Ioanni Pedersen septuagenario dicata* (Copenhagen: Einar Munksgaard, 1953) 219-35; J. Gray, *The Legacy of Canaan* (VTSup 5; Leiden: Brill, 1957) 115-16, 138-40; "Social Aspects of Canaanite Religion," *Volume du Congrès, Genève 1965* (VTSup 15; Leiden: Brill, 1966) 176-85, 192; W. Schmidt, *Königtum Gottes in Ugarit und Israel* (BZAW 80; Berlin: de Gruyter, 1961) 52-54; C.E. L'Heureux, *Rank Among the Canaanite Gods* (HSM 21; Missoula, MT: Scholars, 1979).

[8] See H. Otten, "Ein kanaanäischer Mythus aus Boğazköy," *Mitteilungen des Instituts für Orientforschung* 1 (1953) 125-50, and "Kanaanäische Mythen aus Hattusa-Boğazköy," MDOG 85 (1953) 27-38. An English translation is provided by A. Goetze in *ANET* (3rd ed.) 519. See also H.A. Hoffner, "The Elkunirsa Myth Reconsidered," *Revue hittite et asianique* 76 (1965) 5-16.

[9] "Aṯirat," 248.

[10] *CTA* 36.8. In line three, sheep (š) are offered to El, Baal and Dagan, and in line five, to El, Baal, Asherah, Yamm, and [Baa]l Kanap. Other offerings to Baal, Anat and Yariḫ appear in this list.

[11] *CTA* 30.5. See "Aṯirat," 249, and *El in the Ugaritic Texts* 85-90 for discussion and bibliography.

he also took over his wife."[12] Pope argues that Asherah's infidelity to Elkunirsa is justified on account of his impotence. This impotence is allegedly reflected in *CTA* 23, the birth of Šaḥar and Šalim.[13] By the Iron Age, as reflected in the Hebrew Bible, the transfer of Asherah to Baal is complete: "A. erscheint immer neben Baal, während El keine Rolle mehr spielt."[14] Pope, following Cassuto's suggestion that Ugaritic mythology may have had a parallel to the Greek myth of Kronos's dethronement by Zeus and the Hittite myth of the storm god dethroning Kumarbi,[15] suggests "with great reserve" that the fragmentary

---

[12] *Baal in the Ras Shamra Texts* 77. When commenting on *CTA* 30.5 and 36.8, Kapelrud states, "this seems to indicate that Asherah was partly seen as Il's consort, partly as Baal's."

[13] Pope's treatment is found in *El in the Ugaritic Texts* 37-42, and more recently, "Ups and Downs in El's Amours," *UF* 11 (1979) 701-708. The same consonantal text is read very differently by Cross, *Canaanite Myth* 22-24. Cross states that "the text is a libretto for a cultic drama," and that "it has been badly misunderstood by reason of its impressionistic and repetitious series of scenes." Pope argues that El's impotence is reflected in the poem—he needs the aid of magical rites in order to achieve an erection. The focus of the disagreement between Pope and Cross is the interpretation of the idiom *ḥṭh nḥt* (line 37). Cross takes *ḥṭ* as "bowstave," citing *CTA* 19.1.14, where *ḥṭ* parallels *qšt*, as well as the biblical idiom *nḥt qšt*, "to bend a bow" (2 Sam 22:35 = Ps 18:35). Thus, "El bends his bowstave." Pope reads *ḥṭh* as "his rod," and *nḥt* in its common meaning "to sink." Thus, "El's rod sinks." However, Cross points out that there appear to be both a *nḥt, "to go down," and a *nḥt, "to smooth" or "furbish" (see Akkadian and Arabic cognates). Pope reads the former, though the text has the latter (with *ḥet*). In the parallel colon *ymnn mṭ ydh*, Cross now reads *ymnn* as a Paalel form of the root *MNN*, (no longer a denominative from *yamīn*, "to draw with the right hand," as argued in *Canaanite Myth*) and *mṭ* as "arrow" or "dart" (Hab 3:9, //*qšt*, and *CTA* 3.2.15, 16, *mṭm*//*qšt*). Pope reads *mṭ ydh* as "love-staff" and *ymnn* as "it droops." The meaning of *MNN* is the focus of disagreement. In Arabic it can mean both "to weary" and "be strong" (see *manūn*, "strong," "broken," "weak," "robust" and so on). Cross will argue in a future article that the original meaning of *MNN* is "to strain," "make taut." The secondary meaning would be "to become weak," "weary" (as a result of straining). He will cite Akkadian *manānu*, "sinews," "nerves," and Syriac *minnîn/minnē*, "sinew," "hair," in defense of his position. The cruces of this text remain unresolved. It is certainly clear that El is not impotent; there is intercourse between El and the two goddesses, producing offspring. However, Cross's arguments are not altogether convincing either. The Arabic cognate root *MNN* is simply too ambiguous, and we can assume nothing about its range of meaning in Ugaritic.

[14] "Aṭirat," 249. Day ("Asherah," 391) more or less agrees with Pope, but with some reserve: "Whatever the conclusion of this myth, it does suggest estrangement between Elkunirša (El) and Ašertu (Athirat) and helps shed some light on the background of the OT allusions that associate Baal and Asherah."

[15] *The Goddess Anath* 55-56: "We may conjecture, it seems (although there is no express evidence of this so far in the texts in our possession), that the Canaanites used to relate that at first El ruled over the entire world, but his sons dethroned him and divided the dominion between them."

text in *CTA* 1.5.4-28 may well represent the analogue.[16] The mention of "loins" (*mtn[m]* 12, 14, 25), "accosting" (*hd tngtnh* 4, 17) and "binding" (*t'asrn tr 'il* 22) are cited in this regard.[17]

We may begin our comments with the observation that the texts of the Hebrew Bible alone do not constitute convincing evidence for the thesis that Asherah became the consort of Baal in the Iron Age. In our previous discussion, we observed that the texts which associate Baal with Asherah or her cult symbol are exemplary of deuteronomistic polemic. The association of Aštart with Baal in other deuteronomistic texts represents a more accurate portrayal of Canaanite religion in the Iron Age.[18] Even within the Deuteronomistic History, there is evidence that Asherah was worshiped as the consort of Yahweh in at least some non-deuteronomistic circles (Deut 16:21), not to mention the evidence from the epigraphic corpus. Thus, there is a tension within the Deuteronomistic History between accurate cultic observation (Aštart was worshiped as Baal's consort) and anti-Asherah polemic (people worshiped Asherah as Baal's consort). If it is to be demonstrated that Asherah really became the consort of Baal in Iron Age Canaanite religion, Phoenician or Punic texts that show such an association will have to be found.

In addition to the questionable biblical data, Canaanite mythological lore from the Late Bronze Age is cited in support of the thesis. The key text is the Elkunirsa fragment. There are other, more convincing ways to interpret this text, especially in light of the related Ugaritic mythological material. First, we note that the storm god (Baal) does not act without El's permission. After Asherah has attempted to seduce him, he consults El immediately about what is to be done. El is portrayed as an executive deity in control of the situation and, most important, in control of Baal's behavior. In no sense do we see Baal taking El's

---

[16] Pope, *El in the Ugaritic Texts* 30. Oldenburg (*The Conflict Between El and Ba'al* 123-25) argues that Baal and his allies captured, bound and castrated El on Mt. Ṣapon.

[17] The text is too fragmentary to evaluate with much confidence, and Pope too is wary about speculation. In line 22, *t'asrn tr 'il*, *tr 'il* could be read as the subject following a 2 ms verb with energic suffix or 3 ms suffix instead of the object of the verb. Of course the verb could be read in a number of other ways. Oldenburg would like to read *wǵr* in *wǵr mtny* as a verb rather than "mountain," cognate with Arabic *zarra*, "to cut" (ibid., 185 n.6) Thus, El is castrated in this scene. Considering its fragmentary condition, it is best to put this text aside. Mullen, *The Divine Council* 101-109, provides an analysis of *CTA* 1.5, noting difficulties in interpretation. In his words, "the action is wholly obscure" (105).

[18] Judg 2:13, 10:6; 1 Sam 7:3, 4; 12:10; 1 Kgs 11:5, 33; 2 Kgs 23:13, where she is called "*šiqqûṣ* (abomination) of the Sidonians".

wife away from him by force because he is too weak to stop him. Baal reports Asherah's behavior to her husband. El orders Baal to sleep with her in order to humiliate her: "Go, sleep with her! [Lie with] my [wi]fe and humble her!"[19] They sleep together and Baal insults Asherah: "Of t[hy sons] I slew 77, I slew 88."[20] He is doing precisely what El had ordered. As a result of this affront, Asherah is angry and humiliated, and mourns seven years. After a break in the text, El is addressing Asherah. He turns Baal over to her. She is to deal with him as she pleases. El appears in the end to have reacted negatively to Baal's actions. Unfortunately, the gap in the text does not allow us to know the reasons behind this change. Perhaps Baal's overzealousness to humiliate Asherah is responsible. In any case, Baal is now to be punished by order of El. *IŠTAR* overhears the conversation between El and Asherah and goes off, presumably to warn Baal. In Ullikummi this *IŠTAR* is the sister and ally of Baal, so we may presume that Anat is intended.[21] The fragment ends with El and Asherah sleeping together. Pope does not mention this, but it is an essential observation if we are to interpret the text accurately. The myth hardly suggests that El, old and senile, loses his wife to Baal. On the contrary, the fragment ends with Asherah and El once again together (perhaps we should not even assume they were ever estranged), and a state of severe alienation between the storm god and Asherah. El's alleged impotence is not evident in this text. Not surprisingly, Anat acts as Baal's spy and ally. The one thing that remains unclear is why Asherah attempted to seduce Baal in the first place. It is conceivable that Asherah was frustrated because El was paying more attention to younger goddesses. In other texts, he is involved from time to time with other wives or mistresses.[22] Asherah may have attempted to seduce the storm god in order to spark jeal-

---

[19] Translation of Goetze, *ANET* (3rd ed.) 519; Hoffner, "Elkunirsa Myth," 8; and Otten, "Mythus," 127 render the text similarly.

[20] Goetze, ibid. 519. The slaying of two of Asherah's children is described in *CTA* 6.5.1-4. In *CTA* 4.2.12-26, there is an allusion to Baal and Anat striking the children of Asherah, or at least Asherah's fear that they would do so. Baal and Anat are called *mḫṣy* (**māḫiṣāyya*), "my adversaries."

[21] See Otten, "Mythus," 143 n.59, who notes that Anat flies in the Aqhat epic, suggesting that *IŠTAR* here is Anat. Hoffner, "Elkunirsa Myth," 6 suggests that *IŠTAR* is a combination of both Anat and West Semitic Aštart. I would like to thank Ronald S. Hendel for bringing this to my attention.

[22] In *PE* 1.10.22-23, Astarte is one of El's wives. *CTA* 23 mentions two unnamed goddesses with whom El copulates. This against Cassuto and others who argue that these wives of El are human (*The Goddess Anath* 57). *Ug. V.2.2-4* has been cited by Cross as a text associating El and Aštart, but this is not at all clear (*Canaanite Myth* 21). See our discussion of this text ahead.

ousy in her husband and captivate El's interest once again. In the end, Asherah succeeds, albeit after suffering a bitter humiliation.

This text is helpful in illuminating the prevalent state of tension in Ugaritic mythology between Baal and Anat on the one hand and Asherah and her children on the other. This alienation is illustrated in *CTA* 4.2.12-26. At the approach of Baal and Anat, Asherah is frightened almost to death:

bi-naša'i[23] ' *êneha wa-tipāhunna*
huluki ba' li 'atiratu[24] *kī-ta' īn*
huluki batūlati ' anati
tadrīqa yabamti [lu'mi-mi]
biha pa' nāmi [tattutā]
[ba']danna kislu [tatbur]
[' alênna pa]nūha tadi[' ūf[25]
tiġġaṣū[26] *[pinnātu kis]liha*
'anašā dūta zāri[haf[27]
tišša'u gāha[28] *wa-taṣīhu*
['ê]ka maġaya 'al'iyānu [ba]' lu
'êka maġayat ba[tū]latu ' anatu
māhiṣāyya himā [ma]hiṣā banīya
himā [mukalliyā ṣu]brata 'aryīya

When she lifted her eyes she looked
The coming of Baal Asherah did see
The approach of Maiden Anat
The coming of the kinswoman of the people.
By her, her feet did shake
Behind her, (her) back was shattered
Above, her face broke into a sweat
The joints of her back trembled
Those of her back became weak(?)[29]
She lifted her voice and called,

---

[23] A temporal infinitive. The verb is of the yiqtal type (see below *tišša'u* and BH *yiśśā'*), and the infinitive *něśō'* occurs in Biblical Hebrew.

[24] The text reads erroneously *'attrt* for *'atrt*. See recently G. del Olmo Lete, *Mitos y Leyendas de Canaan. Segun la tradicion de Ugarit* (Institucion San Jeronimo Fuentes de la Ciencia Biblica 1; Madrid: Ediciones Cristiandad, 1981) 195.

[25] From the root *WD'*, "to perspire." See BH *zē'â*, "sweat."

[26] The form here is odd. We should expect a f pl.

[27] See the Hebrew cognates *ṣōhar* "roof," and *ṣohŏrayim*, "noon."

[28] A guess. We vocalize **gāha* on analogy with **śū/śī/śā*. The accusative is required here.

[29] The meaning of *'anš* (**'anašā?*) is unclear. Apparently, the root is *'NŠ*. Hebrew *'NŠ*, "to be weak," is however from etymological *t*, not *š* (thus **'NT > 'NŠ*). A root **'NŠ* does not exist in Semitic. The meaning "weak" seems to fit the context, so we have adopted it, though we note the linguistic difficulties. Others have associated

"Woe! Al'iyan Baal has come,
Woe! The Maiden Anat has arrived.
As for my adversaries,[30] have they struck my children?
Have they made an end of the band of my kin?"

The context of this scene is the approach of Baal and Anat to entreat Asherah to go to El and ask him to grant Baal a temple.

The second text we shall examine is *CTA* 6.1.39-42. The column begins with Anat mourning Baal's death. She buries him and calls on El after elaborate sacrifices:

tišša'u gāha wa-taṣīḥu
tišmaḥū hi{mā}[31] 'aṯiratu wa-banūha
'ilatu wa-ṣubratu 'aryīha
kī-mitu 'al'iyānu ba'lu
kī-ḫalaqa zubūlu ba'lu 'arṣi

She lifted up her voice and called:
"Let them rejoice—Asherah and her children!
Elat and the band of her kin!
For Al'iyan Baal is dead
Indeed the prince, the lord of the earth has perished."

In *CTA* 6.5.1-4, Baal seizes and kills some of Asherah's sons upon his return to kingship. El had asked Asherah for one of her sons to assume Baal's throne after he had died.

In light of this prevailing sense of alienation between Baal and Anat on the one hand and Asherah and her children on the other, one is led to observe that Asherah and Baal really have little to do with each other in Bronze Age mythology, but for the disastrous encounter narrated in the Elkunirsa fragment. When Baal dies, Anat expects Asherah and her children to rejoice. Baal attacks some of Asherah's children when he returns to life. Asherah shows great fear when Baal and Anat approach, alluding to their violent acts against her children, calling them "my adversaries" (lit. "those who strike me," **māḥiṣāyya*).[32] Asherah's position as El's consort is consistent in this lore. Aštart and Anat are Baal's primary associates. The weight of these observations must be considered seriously when we evaluate the formulations of Kapelrud, Pope, Cassuto and

'anš with Arabic *'anisa*, "to be familiar." See the discussion of Maier, *'Ašerah* 9 n.C; KB; and *UT* 3.268.

[30] *mḫṣy, *māḥiṣāyya*, is likely a dual participle with first singular pronominal suffix from the root *MḪṢ*, "to strike," literally "those who strike me."

[31] The text here reads *ht*. The emendation to *h{m}* is Albright's suggestion, *JPOS* 12 (1932) 13 n.44. See also del Olmo Lete, *Mitos* 224-25, n.44.

[32] "Aṯirat," 248. "Der Zweck dieser Gabe ist nicht ganz klar."

Oldenburg. A cumulative view of the Bronze Age mythological material does not suggest that Asherah is lost by El to Baal nor does it even suggest a positive relationship between Asherah and Baal.

The third class of data Pope mentions in support of his thesis are the ritual texts from Ugarit. Pope argues that there is evidence in these texts that Asherah is in the process of being lost to Baal because of the dedication in *CTA* 36.8 (*UT* 9.8), where Baal and Asherah are mentioned together.[33] He also notes the mention of El and Asherah together in *CTA* 30.5 (*UT* 107.5). The mention of two deities together in a dedicatory context does not necessarily indicate that they are paired as consorts, although this is often the case. *CTA* 33.11, 14 (*UT* 5.11, 14) contains a dedication "to Šapaš and Yariḫ" (*lšpš wyrḫ*). In the mythological lore, Yariḫ, the moon god, is paired with Nikkal, the moon goddess, but never with the sun goddess, Šapaš (*CTA* 24 [*UT* 77]).[34] Yet here we have a dedication to Šapaš and Yariḫ, the sun and the moon. This might suggest that in a local cult, Šapaš and Yariḫ are worshiped together as a consort pair, but then again it might suggest nothing of the kind. This type of dedicatory evidence is ambiguous in itself. It seems best to consider such evidence together with the mythological lore extant. Punic dedications also help to illustrate these observations. Though there are numerous dedications to Tannit and Baal Ḥamon (who are indeed a consort pair),[35] there are other dedicatory texts which pair deities not known to be associated in this way, and sometimes two deities of the same sex. Examples include *KAI* 73, "to Aštart and Pygmalion"; *KAI* 81: "to the ladies Aštart and Tannit in Lebanon"; *KAI* 119: "to the lord *šdrp'* and to *mlk'štrt*, lords of Leptis."[36] Sometimes in dedications, whole lists of gods and goddesses appear. This evidence demonstrates that the pairing of deities in dedicatory contexts cannot be cited

---

[33] In Kapelrud's view, this indicates that Baal and El shared Asherah as a consort at this point (*Baal and the Ras Shamra Texts* 77).

[34] In the treaty of Assurnirari V (reverse 6.8), Sîn and Ningal are paired, and precede Šamaš and Aya. The pairing of Yariḫ and Nikkal in West Semitic religion parallels this. J. Fitzmyer, who cites the above treaty, reconstructs S[în and Nikkal] after Šamaš and Nūr in Sefire 1 A 9. The pairing of Šamaš and Aya is found regularly in Akkadian literature. See for example Samsuiluna (Fitzmyer, *The Aramaic Inscriptions of Sefîre* [BibOr 19; Rome: Pontifical Biblical Institute, 1967] 35).

[35] See for example the following in *KAI*: 79.1, 10; 85.1; 86.1; 88.1; 94.1; 97.1; 102.1; 105.1; 137.1 (only Baal appears here, but Baal Ḥamon is obviously intended). In 78.2, Baal Šamêm, Tannit and Baal Ḥamon are mentioned together in a dedication, along with Baal *mgnn*.

[36] *l'dn lšdrp' wlmlk'štrt rbt 'lpqy m's. . .*

as evidence that the named deities are in a consort relationship. Though this is sometimes the case, the evidence suggests that it is often not so. Thus the data can be ambiguous.

Having evaluated the evidence cited to support the hypothesis that Asherah becomes the consort of Baal in Iron Age Canaanite religion, let us move on to a consideration of the data for continuity and conservatism in Canaanite religion. There is abundant evidence for continuity between the religion of the second millennium BCE and that of the first. Canaanite religion on the whole was a conservative phenomenon. We can cite some examples relevant to our topic. First, let us examine the relationship of Aštart and Baal. In Bronze Age mythological texts, Aštart is often portrayed as Baal's consort and ally. We may cite *CTA* 2.1.40, where Aštart prevents Baal from threatening the messengers of Yamm, and *CTA* 2.4.28, where she admonishes him not to harm defeated Yamm.[37] In both cases she is attentive to his best interests. We should also mention her epithet **šimu ba'li*, "the name of Baal," an early example of hypostatization in Canaanite religion, which directly associates her with Baal, as a manifestation of his name essence.[38] Iron Age texts suggest continuity. In the Ešmunazor inscription (*KAI* 14.18), Aštart's archaic epithet *šm b'l* occurs once again. In the lore of Sanchuniathon, Aštart and Baal (Zeus) rule over the land together with the permission of El (Kronos). Aštart, according to this text, places a bull's head upon her head as a symbol of kingship. This suggests clearly that she is queen alongside Baal who is king, though the word "queen" does not occur in the text.[39]

In the lore of Sanchuniathon, Aštart is associated with both Baal and El. She is Baal's consort (*PE* 1.10.31), but also a wife of El, for whom she bears seven daughters and two sons (*PE* 1.10.22-23). But is El paired with Aštart in the Ugaritic lore? According to the reading of *Ug. V.*2.2-4 suggested by Virolleaud,

---

[37] *CTA* 2.1.40: **yamīnahu 'ana]tu ta'ḫud / / šam'alahu ta'ḫud 'attartu*. The restoration [Ana]t is conjectural but likely in light of the frequent pairing of Anat and Aštart in these texts. See for example *Ug.V.*1.9 and *CTA* 14.145-46, 291-93. Herdner argues that the available space does not allow for the reconstruction [*'aṯir]at (CTA* 1:8).

[38] *CTA* 16.6.56.

[39] *PE* 1.10.31. *Astartē de hē megistē kai Zeus Dēmarous kai Adōdos, basileus theōn, ebasileuon tēs chōras kronou gnōmē. hē de Astartē epethēken tēi idiai kephalēi basileias parasēmon kephalēn taurou*. Notice how Baal is called both Zeus Demaros and Adados. The Baal epithet *dmrn* is known from Ugarit (*CTA* 4.7.39; *PRUV* 2001.2.8).

and championed by Cross, Caquot and others,[40] Aštart appears with both El and Baal, as El's mistress according to Cross:[41] *'ilu yatibu ba-'attarti <šadī>//'ilu tapat[sic]u ba-haddi rā'iyu//dū yašīru wa-yadammiru ba-kinnāri,* "El is enthroned with Attart <of the field>//El sits as judge with Haddu his shepherd//who sings and plays on the lyre."[42] Unfortunately, this text is ambiguous, and other scholars, most notably B. Margalit, M. Pope, D. Pardee and M.S. Smith, subscribe to an alternative understanding:[43] *'ilu yatibu bi-'attarti// 'ilu tapizu bi-hidri'iyi//dū-yašīru wa-yadammiru,* "The god [*rp'u*] who dwells in Aštaroth//the god who rules in Edrei//who sings and makes music. . . ."[44] Both Pope and Pardee have shown that the idiom *YTB B-* never means "to be enthroned," but is used exclusively for places.[45] The words *'ttrt* and *hdr'y*, taken as personal names by Virolleaud, Cross et al., are to be seen as the common place names Aštaroth and Edrei, a suggestion originally proposed by Margalit.[46] These two towns are the home of Og of Bashan (that is, the Rephaim) according to Josh 12:4; 13:12, 31. The advantages of this reading are obvious, and the weight of the evidence favors it.[47] Even if one were to accept the reading of Virolleaud, Cross, et al., the text is sufficiently ambiguous so that it would not be at all clear that Aštart is paired with El. She could just as easily be with Baal. Thus we do not follow Cross, who uses this text to demonstrate Aštart's associations with El.

Just as we observed continuity into the Iron Age in the case

[40] Virolleaud's translation and remarks appear in *Ug.V.*2, 553; Cross, *Canaanite Myth* 21; A. Caquot, "La tablette *RS* 24.252. Et la question des Rephaïm ougaritiques," *Syria* 53 (1976) 295-304; L'Heureux, *Rank Among the Canaanite Gods* 172, who is reviewed by D. Pardee in *AfO* 28 (1981/82) 265-67 and M. Pope in *BASOR* 251 (1983) 67-68. There are others who subscribe to this view.

[41] Ibid. 21.

[42] Ibid. 21.

[43] Margalit, "A Ugaritic Psalm (*RS* 24.252)," *JBL* 89 (1970) 292-304; Pope, "Notes on the Rephaim Texts," in *Essays on the Ancient Near East in Memory of Jacob Joel Finkelstein,* ed. M. de Jong Ellis (Hamden, CT: Archon, 1977) 170; "The Cult of the Dead at Ugarit," in *Ugarit in Retrospect: Fifty Years of Ugarit and Ugaritic,* ed. G.W. Young (Winona Lake, IN: Eisenbrauns, 1981) 171-72; D. Pardee, "The Preposition in Ugaritic," *UF* 7 (1975) 352; *UF* 8 (1976) 245; M.S. Smith, "Kothar-wa-Ḥasis, the Ugaritic Craftsman God," Ph.D. dissertation, Yale University, 1985, 387-96, 432-34, for extended discussion and bibliography.

[44] Smith, ibid. 419, 446.

[45] Pope, "Notes," 170; Pardee, "Preposition," 352 and 8:245.

[46] "Ugaritic Psalm," 292-304. Other aspects of Margalit's analysis are not convincing.

[47] The idiom *YTB B-* ceases to be a problem; Haddu, which Pope observed is never an A term in poetry, ceases to be an issue here (see Pope, "Cult of the Dead," 159-79). For further discussion, see Smith, "Kothar-wa-Ḥasis," 433-34.

of Baal's relationship with Aštart, so our Iron Age texts suggest that the relationship between El and Asherah remained unchanged. In the Iron Age, however, there are sometimes difficulties identifying El and Asherah. In most Iron Age Phoenician and Punic material, they go by epithets and not by their traditional names. Obviously, we do not accept the view espoused by some scholars that El declines in importance to the point where he does not even appear in most Iron Age texts. On the contrary, the identification of El with Baal Ḥamon, well known from Punic inscriptions and Kilamuwa, is secure. A confident identification of Asherah with Tannit, the consort of Baal Ḥamon, requires more argumentation, and may not be possible. In the case of Sanchuniathon, Kronos is equated with El, and Dione/Rhea are used for Asherah.

We shall begin our discussion with Sanchuniathon. Though Rhea's identification is not immediately transparent, the same cannot be said for Dione. In Greek mythology, she is an Oceanid/Titanid. Her name is likely related to the adjective *diôs, diâ, dión*, "god-like" (see *Diós*, gen. of Zeus). Thus, the name in Sanchuniathon is probably intended to render West Semitic Elat (**'ilat-*), "the goddess" par excellence, a common epithet of Asherah.[48] As we would expect, Dione is consort of Kronos along with Rhea and Astarte/Aphrodite (*PE* 1.10.22, 24). According to Sanchuniathon, Dione is also called Baaltis, and Kronos her husband gave her Byblos (*PE* 1.10.35). Baaltis is a rendering of West Semitic **ba'lat-*, "lady," and this text suggests that the lady of Byblos (*b'lt gbl*), well known from Phoenician inscriptions, is Asherah.[49] In Sanchuniathon and in other first millennium Phoenician texts, Anat is identified with Athena (see *KAI* 42.1).[50] She is the daughter of Kronos (*PE* 1.10.18), and his ally in war against Ouranos. Aštart is known as Astarte or Aphrodite. Who then is Rhea? She is a wife of Kronos (*PE*

---

[48] *CTA* 14.4.201; 15.3.25-26 *'aṭirat*//*'ilat* and so on. The title Elat occurs in Iron Age inscriptions, though less frequently than Tannit. See *CIL* 8.21683 (PN Amatallat, "Maidservant of Elat"); *CIS* 1.243-44, where priests of Elat are named, and *CIS* 1.149, where a temple of Lady Elat is mentioned; *CIS* 1.221, 430, 646, etc., where the PN *ḥt('')lt* occurs. Tyrian coins portray Elat of Tyre (*'lt ṣr*) as a sea goddess riding a ship. See H. Hamburger, "A Hoard of Syrian Tetradrachms and Tyrian Bronze Coins from Gush Ḥalav," *IEJ* 4 (1954) 224 no. 137 (pl. 20, 21), as cited by Cross, *Canaanite Myth* 31.

[49] *KAI* 4, 5, 6, 7, 10. See the remarks of Attridge and Oden in *Philo of Byblos* 91-92 n.132, and Cross, *Canaanite Myth* 28 n.90.

[50] See the detailed discussion of R. du Mesnil du Buisson, *Nouvelles études sur les dieux et les mythes de Canaan* (Etudes préliminaires aux religions orientales dans l'Empire romain 33; Leiden: Brill, 1973) 48-55.

1.10.22), and the mother of seven of his sons (*PE* 1.10.24). According to *PE* 1.10.34, Rhea is the mother of Mouth, who is Môt of Ugaritic myth.[51] In Greek mythology, Rhea is the wife of Kronos. Taking this evidence into account, it is easiest to see in Rhea an Asherah figure. The presence of two Asherah figures in Sanchuniation's lore is not surprising. It reflects the poetic background of the traditions, preserving in prose form the poetic pair Asherah//Elat, familiar from Ugaritic texts. Dione = Elat and Rhea = Asherah.[52]

In Sanchuniathon, El's consorts are Asherah (Rhea/Dione) and Aštart. The picture presented here is little changed from that of the Ugaritic corpus. Nowhere is Dione/Rhea associated with Adados/Demaros/Zeus (=Baal). Aštart, however, is associated with both El and Baal, and there is no clear evidence for this in the Ugaritic corpus. One notable difference between the Ugaritic texts and Sanchuniathon is the less prominent role of Anat in the latter, and the corresponding increase in the prominence of Aštart. This reflects the ascendency of Aštart in the religion of the Iron Age. Curiously, Anat/Athena is not mentioned with Baal in Sanchuniathon. When she is mentioned, she is Kronos's daughter (*PE* 1.10.18, 32). The Sanchuniathon material suggests that Aštart has become Baal's primary consort in Iron Age Phoenician religion.[53] This comes as no surprise, con-

---

[51] See Attridge and Oden, *Philo of Byblos* 91, n.131.

[52] See further the discussion of Cross, *Canaanite Myth* 28. We do not agree with those who would identify Dione/Baaltis with Anat (de Moor, "'ăshērāh," 440). There is no evidence to support this.

[53] A careful comparison of the traditions attributed to Sanchuniathon with older sources of Canaanite myth suggests strongly the historical value of the "Phoenician History" as a source for reconstructing the development of Canaanite religion to the end of the first millennium BCE. The existence of the historical person Sanchuniathon is open to debate, as recent contributions demonstrate, but we find it difficult not to agree with those scholars who have argued for the historical value of the source per se. See recently J. Barr, "Philo of Byblos and his 'Phoenician History,'" *BJRL* 57 (1974) 17-68, and Attridge and Oden, *Philo of Byblos* 5-9. Both Albright and Eißfeldt argued that Sanchuniathon was a historical person who lived long before Philo, his reporter. Albright (*Archaeology and the Religion of Israel* 70-71) argued that Sanchuniathon must have lived in the mid-first millennium. Eißfeldt (*Sanchunjaton von Berut und Ilumilku von Ugarit* [Beiträge zur Religionsgeschichte des Altertums 5; Halle: Niemeyer, 1952] 68) argued for a date in the second millennium. When considering the two, the latter view seems far less cogent. It is also possible that Sanchuniathon lived in the Hellenistic or Roman period, as Attridge and Oden suggest. Whether Sanchuniathon lived or not, and if so when, is not a focal issue for us. The lore attributed to him and the question of its value is central. We believe that this lore reflects the developments in Iron Age Canaanite religion as witnessed elsewhere. For example, the role and importance of Aštart in the first millennium, by all accounts, increases dramatically. In "The

sidering the importance of Aštart in first millennium epigraphic texts.

In most Iron Age Phoenician and Punic materials, El is called by the epithet Baal Ḥamon. The identification of El with Baal Ḥamon is secure. Benno Landsberger suggested it in 1948, and others, notably F.M. Cross, have presented a convincing case for it.[54] As Landsberger pointed out, the main texts to be noted in this regard are the Zinjirli dynastic inscriptions of Kilamuwa (*KAI* 24), Hadad (*KAI* 214) and Panammu (*KAI* 215). Kilamuwa, to be dated to the last quarter of the ninth century, is written in the Phoenician language and names three major gods: *b ' l ṣmd*, *b ' l ḥmn*, and *rkb'l*, the dynastic lord (*b ' l bt*).[55] In the Aramaic Hadad inscription, Hadad, El and *rkb'l* are named in descending order, along with Šamaš and Rešep.[56] Note also the Panammu inscription, where Hadad, El, *rkb'l*, Šamaš and all the gods of Ya'dî are named.[57] From the order of the names alone,

Phoenician History," she is Baal's consort and plays a significant role. Anat, who is seldom mentioned in Phoenician or Punic inscriptions, is mentioned only twice in "The Phoenician History," and her role is certainly less significant than it was in Bronze Age myth. We could cite numerous other examples. For additional bibliography and detailed commentary, see the recent contribution of A.I. Baumgarten, *The Phoenician History of Philo of Byblos. A Commentary* (Etudes préliminaires aux religions orientales dans l'Empire romain 89; Leiden: Brill, 1981).

[54] Landsberger, *Sam'al* (Ankara: Druckerei der Türkischen historischen Gesellschaft, 1948) 47 n.117. Landsberger bases his assertion on the comparison of the series of gods in Kilamuwa and in Hadad/Panammu. See Cross, *Canaanite Myth* 10, 24-28, including analysis of the meaning of the epithet Baal Ḥamon.

[55] Lines 15-16. For one view of the symbolism of the Zinjirli stelae, see Y. Yadin, "Symbols of Deities at Zinjirli, Carthage and Hazor," in *Near Eastern Archaeology in the Twentieth Century. Essays in Honor of Nelson Glueck*, ed. J. Sanders (Garden City: Doubleday, 1970) 199-231.

[56] Lines 2-3, 11.

[57] Line 22. The Hadad inscription of Zinjirli is probably to be dated to the early eighth century, and the Panammu inscription to ca. 730. They are written in a dialect of Old Aramaic which preserves some archaic features shared in common with Canaanite. Against J. Friedrich, *Phönizisch-Punische Grammatik* (AnOr 32; Rome: Pontifical Biblical Institute, 1951) 153-62, who argued for a distinct language "Jaudisch." See among others the criticisms of Cross and Freedman, *Early Hebrew Orthography* 61-64; E.Y. Kutscher, "Aramaic," in *Current Trends in Linguistics* 6 (1970) 347-412; P. Dion, *La langue de Ya'udi* (Waterloo, ONT: CPASRC, 1974). The vocalization **ya'udî* is to be rejected. The correct vocalization is likely **ya'dî* or **yadiya* for this period. See N.Na'aman, "Sennacherib's 'Letter to God' on his Campaign to Judah," *BASOR* 214 (1974) 25-39, who argues against Rost's reading *[I]z-ri-ja-u māt(KUR) Ja-u-di*. Na'aman suggests the better reading *ina biri[t mi]ṣrija u māt(KUR) Jaudi*, where Azriyau disappears completely. Yaudi here is clearly Judah, not the Sam'al kingdom. The mention of Azekah ([URU]*A-za-qa-a*, line 5) and Philistia (line 11) make this clear enough. For the alternative view, see M.C. Astour, "Ya'udi," *IDBSup* 975.

b'l ṣmd of Kilamuwa should be identified with Hadad. Both are named first. This identification makes perfect sense in light of what we know about Hadad-Baal. The name *b'l ṣmd* should be vocalized **ba'l ṣimd*, "the lord of the war-club."[58] Baal is often portrayed holding a club,[59] and in his defeat of Yamm, two magic war-clubs fashioned by Kôṯar-wa-Ḥasis, **'āy-yamarrī* and **yagarriš*, play a prominent role (*CTA* 2.4.11-27). In light of Baal's well-known association with the war club, "lord of the chariot harness" is a less appealing but nonetheless possible translation. The dynastic lord **rākib'il* is more difficult to identify.[60] His name means "El's rider." This leaves only *b'l ḥmn*, second in order in Kilamuwa, corresponding to El of the Hadad inscription (2, 11) and the Panammu inscription (22). Other evidence confirms the equation El = *b'l ḥmn*, which is suggested by the Zinjirli series. Diodorus Siculus (among other classical writers) describes the cult of child sacrifice in Carthage dedicated to Kronos, and mentions the myth of Kronos sacrificing his own children.[61] Versions of this myth are preserved in Sanchuniathon (*PE* 1.10.33-34, 44). The many Punic child dedications to Baal Ḥamon suggest strongly the equation El/Kronos = *b'l ḥmn*. For the vocalization **ba'l ḥamōn* and a discussion of the meaning of the epithet, see Cross's treatment.[62]

Baal Ḥamon's consort in the Punic world is *tnt*, best vocalized **tannit*, who is to be identified with Asherah according to the arguments of Cross, R. Oden and others.[63] On at least one

[58] Cross, *Canaanite Myth* 10. Yadin ("Symbols," 213) rejects this interpretation.

[59] *ANEP* 481, 484 (most likely representations of Baal with raised right hand, which would have held a lightning bolt, and left hand extended, which probably held a war-club); 490 (figurine has raised right hand with club, and a stylized lightning bolt in left hand); 494, 496 (may be representations of Baal with club and shield).

[60] Cross (*Canaanite Myth* 10 n.32) suggests that *rkb'l* is possibly the moon god Yariḥ. This is based on the symbolism appearing on the stela.

[61] *Library of History* 13.86.3; 20.14.1, 4-7. See also Sophocles, *Andromeda*, 122. A thorough discussion of child sacrifices mentioned in classical sources is to be found in P. Mosca, "Child Sacrifice in Canaanite and Israelite Religion" (Ph.D. dissertation, Harvard University, 1975).

[62] *Canaanite Myth* 26-28. A recently published amulet from the Tyre area records a dedication to Baal Ḥamon and Baal Ṣapon. Baal Ḥamon is here distinguished from Baal Ṣapon. See P. Bordreuil, "Attestations inédites de Melqart, Baal Ḥamon et Baal Ṣaphon à Tyr," in *Studia Phoenicia IV* (Namur: Société des études classiques, 1986) 77-86.

[63] Cross, *Canaanite Myth* 32-33, and recently Weinfeld, "Kuntillet 'Ajrud," 125, who accepts the identification of Tannit and Asherah, and believes Asherah was a sea goddess. Cross explains the development of Tannit's name thus: **tannintu* > **tannittu* > **tannit*, "the serpent lady," through expected assimilation, loss of case ending and loss of final doubling. See *tannīn*, "dragon," an epithet of Yamm in

occasion, Aštart too is associated (indirectly) with Baal Ḥamon, which comes as no surprise.[64] Other scholars have argued that Tannit is to be identified with Anat (W.F. Albright,[65] F.L. Benz,[66] F.O. Hvidberg-Hansen[67]) or Aštart (L. Stager,[68] G. Garbini,[69] S. Moscati,[70] D. Harden[71]). If, as we argue, Baal Ḥamon is El, we would expect his consort Tannit either to be

CTA 3.3.37, which appears also in the Hebrew Bible (Isa 27:1; 51:9 and so on). Punic Tennit (thenneith, thinith) can be explained by the shift in Phoenician of *a > e (Friedrich, Phönizisch-Punische Grammatik par. 75b). As Oden has pointed out, no convincing etymology for Tinit or Tennit has yet been proposed (against Donner-Röllig, KAI 2.90), though *tannit can be explained in a cogent manner (De Syria Dea, 92, n.220). See also J.B. Peckham, The Development of the Late Phoenician Scripts (Harvard Semitic Studies 20; Cambridge: Harvard University, 1968) 129 n.74. Cross has argued that tnt is an archaic epithet, and is attested in two proto-Sinaitic inscriptions, paralleled by ḏt bṭn (*ḏāt baṭni), "the one of the serpent," and lb't (*labi'tu), "the lion lady." All are used of Asherah (see "The Origin and Early Evolution of the Alphabet," Eretz Israel 8 [1967] 8*-24*). Many scholars have suggested non-Semitic explanations for Tin(n)it/Tennit. Röllig ("Tinnit," WMyth 1:311) offers this comment: "Der Name selbst ist bisher ohne Erklärung, vielleicht libyschen Ursprungs. . . ." F.O. Hvidberg-Hansen argued recently that tnt is to be derived from Anat plus Berber t prefix with elision of the ayin (La déesse Tnt, un étude sur la religion canaanéo-punique [2 vols.; Copenhagen: Gad, 1979] 103-105). This argument seems overly complex and unlikely, particularly when a strong case can be made for the West Semitic background of the name. Likewise the explanations of F. Løkkegaard (in his review of Hvidberg-Hansen, UF 14 [1982] 137), who derives tnt from 'atān ("ass"), and F. Görg ("Zum Namen der punischen Göttin 'Tinnit,' " UF 11 [1979] 303-306), who restates the old view that tnt is to be derived from Egyptian Neith plus feminine deictic. The DN is now attested in mainland Phoenicia on the Sarepta Plaque published by Pritchard (see n.68). This indicates that it is surely West Semitic. See now Day, "Asherah," 396-97.

[64] KAI 19. A dedication to Aštart "in the sanctuary of the god Ḥamon" (b'šrt 'l ḥmn).

[65] Yahweh and the Gods of Canaan 130, 134-35, and n.63.

[66] Personal Names in the Phoenician and Punic Inscriptions (Studia Pohl 8; Rome: Pontifical Biblical Institute, 1972) 429-30.

[67] La déesse Tnt. See Day, "Asherah," 397, who believes that Tannit is Anat or a deity other than Anat, Asherah or Aštart.

[68] L. Stager and S. Wolff, "Child Sacrifice at Carthage—Religious Rite or Population Control?" Biblical Archaeology Review 10.1 (1984) 31-51. See p. 45, where the Sarepta plaque mentioning tnt 'štrt is discussed. On the Sarepta plaque, see J. Pritchard, "The Tanit Inscription from Sarepta," in Phönizier im Westen, ed. H.G. Niemeyer (Madrider Beiträge 8; Mainz: Zabern, 1982) 83-92, and Recovering Sarepta, A Phoenician City (Princeton: Princeton University, 1978) 104-107, 131-48, especially 148. Pritchard believes that it is more likely that there is an implied wa- conjunction between tnt and 'štrt, so that the shrine would have been dedicated to both goddesses.

[69] V. Bonello et al., Missione archeologica italiana a Malta, I (Rome: University of Rome, 1964) 83-89 pl. 26, and 94-96.

[70] The World of the Phoenicians (New York: Praeger, 1968) 139, 193.

[71] The Phoenicians (London: Thames and Hudson, 1962) 87.

Asherah or Aštart, since these two goddesses are associated with
El as his consorts in Sanchuniathon, and Asherah is his consort in
the Ugaritic materials. Anat is never El's consort.[72] An examination of the evidence suggests that Aštart is not to be identified
with Tannit. Whereas the name Asherah never occurs in the
western Mediterranean of the first millennium, the name Aš-
tart/Astarte is quite common alongside Tannit. This suggests
that Tannit is not Aštart. The distinction between Tannit and
Aštart is actually established in *KAI* 81.1, an inscription from
Carthage where new holy places are dedicated "to the ladies,
Aštart and Tannit in Lebanon" (*lrbt l'štrt wltnt blbnn*). Obviously, they are not the same goddess. That Aštart's cult was significant in Carthage is attested by the numerous personal names
incorporating the theophoric element *'štrt* found in Carthagin-
ian inscriptions.[73] The Tas Silg data cited by Garbini and Moscati in their attempts to identify Tannit and Aštart are thus less
than convincing, and can be interpreted differently.[74]

L. Stager argued recently that Tannit and Aštart were identified by the seventh century in Phoenicia proper based on the
evidence of the Sarepta plaque, which is a dedication to
tnt'štrt.[75] This kind of combination of two deities into a new
fusion-hypostasis is not unusual in Canaanite religion. Tannit-
Aštart should be viewed as a hypostasis with independent existence both from Tannit and from Aštart, comparable to Aršap-
Melqart (*KAI* 72 A 1),[76] Ešmun-Aštart (*CIS* 1.245), Ešmun-

---

[72] See note 82 for a discussion of *CTA* 23 *'atrt wrhm(y)*. It seems very likely that
this is a compound name for Asherah. In no way is it clear that *rhm(y)* is Anat, nor
does the text indicate that the two wives mentioned later in the seduction scene
are Asherah and Anat. The wives are unnamed in that scene, which is unrelated to
the scene in which *'atrt wrhm(y)* appear(s).

[73] Peckham, *The Development* 121 and n.33. From Carthage, there are 800
names (approximately) with Aštart as theophoric element, third in total number
behind only Baal and Melqart.

[74] Cross, *Canaanite Myth* 30: "These data suggest strongly that at Tas Silg we
must construe the mixture of dedications to *'Aštart* and to *Tannit* as evidence that
the temple originally was dedicated to both, and perhaps to the triad *'Ēl* and his
two wives." The Tas Silg temple was dedicated to Hera/Juno. Tannit is commonly
identified with Hera/Juno, but we note that Aštart, on at least one occasion, is identified with Juno as well (Pyrgi, *KAI* 277). For Aštart we would expect Aphrodite.
The key to a solution to the problem may well lie in the fact that Hera/Juno could
be identified both with Tannit and with Aštart (on occasion), and thus a temple
dedicated to Hera/Juno could be dedicated to both Semitic goddesses at once.

[75] "Child Sacrifice," 45.

[76] *l'dn l'ršp mlqrt mqd[š]*, "To the lord, to 'Aršap-Melqart, a sanctuary. . . ." Donner and Röllig note how common such combinations are, especially in the latter
half of the first millennium. They mention *mlqrt ṣd* (*CIS* 1.256), and *ṣd tnt* (*CIS*
1.247, 248, 249). See *KAI* 2.89 for their comments. They also note the fact that the

Melqart (*CIS* 1.16, 23, 24), and Anatyahû of Elephantine according to some scholars.[77] We should not view the Sarepta plaque as evidence that Tannit and Aštart have lost their separate identities or that they were two names for the same goddess all along. We can cite evidence to demonstrate that the combination deities were thought of as having a separate existence from the deities whose names they carry. The deity *mlk ' štrt* (**milk/mulk ' aštart*) is treated grammatically as a male,[78] and Anatyahû, whether a fusion of Yahweh and Anat or the Sign/Providence of Yahweh, is mentioned in the same sentence as Yahweh. Mulkaštart and Anatyahû do not replace Aštart and Yahweh in their respective pantheons.

W.F. Albright argued that Tannit is to be identified with Anat.[79] He based his case on a number of common epithets shared by Tannit and Anat. He identified Derketô of Ascalon, who shares Tannit's epithet **panê ba ' l*, "the face of Baal,"[80]

combination types male + male, and female + male are attested. With Tannit ' ăstart, we now have the type female + female.

[77] See A. Cowley, *Aramaic Papyri of the Fifth Century B.C.* (Oxford: Clarendon, 1923) no. 44.3, where Anatyahû is mentioned with Yahweh (*yhw*) and the *msgd'* (?) in reference to an oath. The *msgd'* is often taken to mean "temple" in light of Arabic *masjid*, "mosque." See Nabatean *msgd'* and Mandean *masgda/masgida*. It may however mean altar or stela. See the discussions of B. Porten, *Archives from Elephantine* (Berkeley and Los Angeles: University of California, 1968) 155; M.H. Silverman, *Religious Values in the Jewish Proper Names at Elephantine* (AOAT 217; Neukirchen-Vluyn: Neukirchener/Kevelaer: Butzon & Bercker, 1985) 230; J.T. Milik, "Les papyrus araméens d'Hermoupolis et les cultes syro-phéniciens en Egypte perse," *Bib* 48 (1967) 577-80. In Cowley no. 22.123-25, Yahweh, *'šmbyt'l* and *' ntbyt'l* are mentioned together. Anatyahû is not to be seen as Yahweh's consort at Elephantine, as is so often assumed. Albright (*Archaeology and the Religion of Israel* 162-68) argued that Anatyahû should be understood as a hypostasis, the "providence of Yahweh," where *' anat* would be an Aramaic common noun meaning "time," "destiny," or "providence," comparable to Hebrew *' ēt* (< ** ' int-*). See Aramaic *' antā'*, and Akkadian *ittu*, "sign" or "omen." See also the personal name *' antotîyāh*, "Yahweh is my providence," in 1 Chr 8:24. We understand the oath as one taken by Yahweh, the temple or altar, and the "providence of Yahweh," analogous to the "name of Yahweh" in deuteronomistic theology, "the face/presence of Baal" in the expression Tannit *panê ba ' l*, and so on. The occurrence of *' ntbyt'l* and such parallel figures as *'šmbyt'l* in no. 22.123-25, suggest that *' anat* here is a common noun. See also Milik's treatment, ibid. 567, where a similar conclusion regarding *' ntyhw* is reached.

[78] *KAI* 19.2/3; 71: *l'dn l' zz mlk ' štrt wl' bdm*, where *-m* is a Punic 3ms suffix on plural *' bd*, "his servants." See *qlm*, "his voice," in 77.3/4 and *'mm*, "his mother," in 123.3 The suffix *-m* is attested in addition to the more frequent *-y* or *-'*. See Friedrich-Röllig, *Phönizisch-Punische Grammatik* (2nd ed.; AnOr 46; Rome: Pontifical Biblical Institute, 1970) par. 112.

[79] *Yahweh and the Gods of Canaan* 130, 134-35 and n.63.

[80] A title indicating that on at least one level, the goddess was seen as a hypostasis of an aspect of her consort Baal Hamon.

with Anat, based on his interpretation of her name (=*darkat-, "dominion"), an element of an epithet of Anat at Ugarit (*ba ʿlatu darkati, "the lady of dominion").[81] He noted that Tannit is called *Virgo* or *Juno Caelestis*, "the Heavenly Virgin" or "the Heavenly Juno," comparable to Anat's epithet *batūlatu ʿanatu*. Albright proposed that Anat's original full name was *ʿanat panê baʿl*. Thus, according to his reconstruction, Anat = Derketô = Tannit. There are however problems with this thesis. If Tannit = Anat, and Baal Ḥamon = El, there should be some convincing evidence somewhere that El and Anat were associated as consorts, and there is none. Thus, this identification would involve positing a probably hitherto unattested pairing of El and Anat as consorts.[82] This identification is difficult on methodological grounds. Though Albright's understanding of Derketô's name is correct,[83] Anat's epithet *baʿlatu darkati* from Ugarit does not necessarily suggest that Derketô is Anat. The epithets "dominion" and "lady of dominion" are not exactly the same. "Dominion" like "mistress" (*bʿlt*) or "lady" (*rbt*) is not reserved for a single goddess.[84] Cross has pointed out that

---

[81] *Ug.V.*2.6-7.

[82] In *CTA* 23, we read of El's intercourse with two unnamed wives, which leads to the birth of Šaḥar and Šalim, followed by the "goodly gods" (*ʿilm nʿmm*), who suck the nipples of the breasts of Asherah. Previous to these episodes, the designation *ʾatrt wrhm(y)* occurs (23.13, 28) and *rhmy* alone in 23.16. Some scholars have argued that *rhm(y)* here is Anat, since Anat bears the epithet in *CTA* 6.2.27 (see Kapelrud, *Baal in the Ras Shamra Texts* 70; Oldenburg, *The Conflict Between El and Baʿal* 88). Identification of *rhm(y)* of *CTA* 23 with Anat is possible, however an epithet like **rahmu* or **rahmayyu* is easily conceivable for Asherah, the mother goddess par excellence. Mullen (*The Divine Council* 18 n.22) has argued that *ʾatiratu-wa-rahmu/-ayyu* should be seen as a compound name for Asherah, comparable to such divine names as *kôṯar-wa-ḥasis*, or *qudšu-wa-ʾamraru*. In any case, the two goddesses impregnated by El in the text should not be equated necessarily with *ʾatiratu wa-rahmu/-ayyu* of the earlier scene. There is no evidence in *CTA* 23 that the two scenes and their goddesses are connected in any way. Oden (*De Syria Dea* 84-85) discusses the problem, noting that only Asherah may be meant by *ʾatiratu-wa-rahmu/-ayyu*. Anat is Baal's partner in other texts from Ugarit. See *CTA* 10.3.20-23, which however is poorly preserved. Anat bears a child for Baal, described as an ox (**alpu*) and a heifer (**yapattu*, see Arabic *yafanat*) in 10.3.3-4, and in 21-22, 36-37 a bull (**ibīru*) and an ox (**riʾmu*). At this Baal rejoices. In *CTA* 5.5.18-22, Baal mates with a cow (**ʿiglatu*), which Mullen (29 n.50) assumes is Anat. The fragmentary *CTA* 11 suggests the intercourse of Baal and Anat as well. These animal names may well refer to warriors or nobility. See the comments of Oden, ibid. 82 n.178, and P. Miller, "Animal Names as Designations in Ugaritic and Hebrew," *UF* 2 (1970) 177-86.

[83] "Dominion."

[84] *rbt* (**rabbatu*), "lady" or "mistress," is applied to several goddesses: Asherah (*CTA* 4.2.28; 4.3.27; 4.4.31; 6.1.47, 53 and so on); Tannit and Aštart (*KAI* 81.1); Aštart (*KAI* 14.15); the Lady of Byblos (*KAI* 10) and Šapaš (*CTA* 23.54; 16.1.36). *bʿlt*

the marine features of Derketô suggest Asherah, since she is the only great goddess in West Semitic religion associated with the sea.[85] In light of this, the name Derketô is hardly sufficient evidence on which to base the identification of Tannit. An examination of other Tannit epithets cited by Albright suggests that epithets are not the most reliable class of evidence to use in the identification of deities. The association with the heavens (*Virgo/Juno Caelestis*) is not reserved for Anat in West Semitic religion. In Ešmunazor (*KAI* 14.16), Aštart is called "Aštart of the Awesome Heavens" (*šmm 'drm*), and in Egypt, all three great goddesses were called "lady of heaven" (*nb.t p.t*).[86] Tannit's epithet *nutrix* ("wet nurse") could be applied as easily to Asherah as to Anat. In "Kirta" we read of Hurriya, "She will bear *yṣb* the boy//He will suck the milk of Asherah//Suck the breast of the Virgin Anat//The wet-nurses [of the gods]."[87] Tannit's epithet *'m*, "mother," suggests Asherah[88] though Aštart is also identified as a mother in Punic names (see the common *'m 'štrt*, **'im(i) 'aštart*). Since Aštart cannot be Tannit, *'m* suggests Asherah. Anat is never called "mother" in first millennium texts, though at Ugarit, names compounding Anat and *'m* occur. Cross pointed out that Tannit is sometimes identified with Ops (=Rhea), consort of Saturn (=Kronos), suggesting again Asherah.[89] Tannit's epithets at times suggest Asherah, at times Anat, at times Aštart, at times any of the three. Thus, for the most part, epithets are an ambiguous class of data. To identify Tannit with any assurance, we must look beyond epithets.

The evidence in favor of Tannit's identification with Asherah can be summarized as follows: (1) She is the main consort of Baal Ḥamon/El. Only Asherah and Aštart qualify here, and Aš-

---

(**ba' latu*), "lady" or "mistress," is applied to Anat (*Ug. V.*2.6-7) and the Lady of Byblos. In like manner, **ba' l*, "lord," is applied to a number of gods.

[85] *Canaanite Myth* 31. He mentions Asherah's servant Qudšu-wa-'Amraru, "the fisherman of Asherah" (**daggayyu 'aṭirati; CTA* 3.6.10), as well as Asherah/Elat's portrayal as a sea goddess on Tyrian coinage.

[86] See Stadelmann, *Syrisch-Palästinensische Gottheiten* 88-96 on Anat; 96-110 on Aštart; 110-23 on Qudšu, and see Olyan, "Queen of Heaven," *UF* 19 (1988), forthcoming.

[87] *CTA* 15.2.25-28; *tld yṣb ǵlm//ynq ḥlb 'a[t]rt//mṣṣ ṯd btlt ['nt]//mšnq. . . .*

[88] Asherah is the mother, the "creatress of the gods" (**qāniyatu 'ilīma; CTA* 4.1.23; 8.2; 4.3.26, 30; 4.4.32; 4.3.35). However, note the common Phoenician name *'im(i) 'aštart*, "Aštart is (my) mother." See Benz, *Personal Names* 62, for occurrences of this name. Tannit is called "mother" in *CIS* 1.195, 196, 380. It is odd that there are no attested personal names in the Phoenician-Punic corpus which describe Tannit as a mother, nor are there many references in texts to her assumption of this role.

[89] *Canaanite Myth* 32.

tart must be excluded based on the evidence of *KAI* 81.1 and other considerations already discussed. This leaves Asherah. (2) The name Asherah never occurs in the Punic west or for that matter in first millennium Canaanite texts, though it is found in the Hebrew Bible. Tannit occurs prominently beside Baal Ḥamon. Aštart and Anat occur. Why not Asherah too? The evidence of the Hebrew Bible and epigraphic corpus certainly shows that she was worshiped during the first millennium. Is Tannit the popular epithet of Asherah in the Iron Age, especially in the western Phoenician colonies? This seems very likely.[90] This would explain why the name Asherah is nowhere to be found in Iron Age Canaanite texts. (3) Derketô of Ascalon, who bears Tannit's epithet *panê ba ʻ l* (*phanē balos*), has prominent marine associations which suggest strongly Asherah, as Cross has argued.[91] The epithet *panê ba ʻ l*, not associated with any other goddesses, suggests that Tannit and Derketô are the same goddess. We are assuming that the "*ba ʻ l*" of this epithet is Baal Ḥamon. The sign of Tannit occurs on a number of *phanē balos* coins from Ascalon.[92] Tannit, like Derketô, is portrayed with marine associations.[93] The hypostatized "face" or "presence" is associated with El in Canaanite religion (see the place names *pĕnîʼēl* and *pĕnûʼēl* in the Hebrew Bible). It is never associated with Baal Hadad as far as we know. This may suggest that the bearer of this epithet is the consort of El/Baal Ḥamon. (4) Though Tannit shares some epithets with Anat and Aštart,

---

[90] Ibid. 33.

[91] In Diodorus 2.4.2-6, Derketô is distinguished from Aphrodite (Astarte). She has the head of a woman and the body of a fish (Cross, *Canaanite Myth* 31). On *pn b ʻ l*/*phanē balos* see in addition *KAI* 78.2; 175.2 and 176.2-3.

[92] On the sign of Tannit on the *phanē balos* coins, see G.F. Hill, *Catalogue of the Greek Coins of Palestine* (Catalogue of the Greek Coins in the British Museum 27; London: British Museum, 1914) 18, 107, 187, etc.

[93] The sign of Tannit, a stylized image of a woman in a long dress with upraised arms, appears on Punic stelae often with dolphins or fish, suggesting a marine goddess. See A.M. Bisi, *Le stele puniche* (Studi Semitici 27; Rome: Istituto di studi del vicino oriente, 1967) fig. 32, 74, and plates xxvi.3, xxxiii.1. Often, the disk and crescent appear, as well as birds. On the sign of Tannit, see Moscati, "L'origine de 'segno di Tanit,' " in *Accademia Nazionale dei Lincei: Rendiconti*, series 8, 27:371-74, and G. Benigni, "Il 'segno di Tanit' in Oriente," *Revista di studi fenici* 3 (1975) 17-18. Tannit's associations with the cult of human sacrifice in the west deserve more attention from scholars. Many Punic *mlk* vows include Tannit with Baal Ḥamon, and fig. 32 (mentioned above) shows a man with right hand raised in a gesture of blessing (a priest?) holding a child beneath symbols of Tannit and Baal Ḥamon (fish, crescent and disk). Fig. 31 shows a man with a child flanked by crescent and disk symbols on either side. The motif is repeated in fig. 36, where palms appear on either side of the priest and a sign of Tannit appears at the top of the stela. The symbolism suggests Tannit's intimate connections with child sacrifice.

which are not normally associated with Asherah (e.g. *virgo*), the epithet *'m*, "mother," suggests Asherah, "the Creatress of the gods."[94] The same applies to the identification of Tannit with Ops in certain texts. The epithet *nutrix* suggests Asherah as much as Anat. (5) R. Oden has pointed out the significance of various stylized trees found in Tannit symbolism for the identification of Tannit with Asherah.[95] These trees appear with the sign of Tannit in a number of stelae.[96] Oden argues insightfully that the caduceus and palm of Tannit are related to the asherah of the Hebrew Bible. The use of trees, especially the palm, as Tannit symbols suggests strongly the identification of Tannit and Asherah. Compare the stylized palm tree (flanked by two ibexes, poised above the back of a lion) on Kuntillet Ajrûd pithos A, which is surely an asherah. (6) An examination of personal names from the Phoenician-Punic corpus tends on the whole to support the equation Tannit = Asherah. Aštart names are ubiquitous, Anat names are attested,[97] but nowhere is Asherah attested as a theophoric element in a name. Of course Tannit names are attested, and here we believe is the solution to the problem.[98] Tannit is probably the popular epithet of Asherah in the Phoenician-Punic world of the first millennium.

The identification of Tannit with Hera/Juno in some texts really tells us little. We should have expected identification with Aphrodite if Tannit were Aštart,[99] or with Athena if she were Anat.[100] As it stands, the identification with Ops (=Rhea) in some texts suggests Asherah.[101] Hera/Juno has no Semitic coun-

[94] For a likely biblical allusion to Asherah as mother goddess, see Olyan, "The Cultic Confessions of Jer 2, 27a," *ZAW* 99 (1987) 254-59.

[95] *De Syria Dea* 151-55. Both the palm and the caduceus are represented.

[96] Bisi, *Le stele puniche* fig. 51, 52, 53. Figure 51 shows a palm with, as it were, two signs of Tannit growing or sprouting out of its base. Figure 52 is similar, though more stylized. Figure 53 shows a sign of Tannit sprouting two blossoms from its base. See also fig. 29. Figure 36 shows two caduceus representations and two palms, with a priestly figure with right hand raised in a gesture of blessing and child (?) in left hand standing between them. At the top of the stela is the sign of Tannit. Figures 70 and 91 are also noteworthy.

[97] *'bd 'nt* (*CIS* 1.3781.1/2; 4563.3; 5550.1/2) and the misspelled *'nt* (*CIS* 1.4976.1), *'bd 'nt* (*CIS* 1.4562.1/2; 4959.1/2).

[98] *'štnt* (*CIS* 1.542.3), *bdtnt* (*CIS* 1.165.1), *'bdtnt* (*CIS* 1.116.1; 501.4; 975.5/6; 2720.2, 3; 4906.3/4; 4978; 5679.2/3), *'ztnt* (*CIS* 1.2026.2).

[99] The identification of Astarte with Aphrodite is common. See *PE* 1.10.32 (*tēn de Astartēn phoinikes tēn Aphroditēn einai legousin*), and J. Fitzmyer, "The Phoenician Inscription from Pyrgi," *JAOS* 86 (1966) 285-97, especially 288 on the usual identification of Astarte and Aphrodite. In Pyrgi (*KAI* 277), the Etruscan text has *unial astres* ("Juno-Astarte"), an odd identification.

[100] *PE* 1.10.18; 1.10.32-33; *KAI* 42.1.

[101] See *CIL* 8.2670, 16527, 26240, as cited by S. Gsell, *Histoire ancienne de*

terpart (the name Hera does not occur in Sanchuniathon).

On the whole, the evidence in favor of identifying Tannit with Asherah is strong, though difficulties remain. Tannit epithets like *virgo* give pause. It may be best to see in Tannit an Asherah figure who has, over time, assimilated some of the epithets of the other great goddesses. Epithets and even some characteristics of the great goddesses were to some extent fluid. Aštart, who is never a mother goddess at Ugarit, is one in the first millennium, as the lore of Sanchuniathon and personal names like *'im(i)'aštart* indicate. In New Kingdom Egypt, we observe fluidity of epithets (and some attributes) with regard to all three great goddesses. With the identification Tannit = Asherah, we may have more evidence of the continuity of association between El and Asherah down to the end of the first millennium.

We observed that in the lore of Sanchuniathon, Asherah (Rhea/Dione) and Aštart are associated with El (Kronos) while Aštart is also Baal's consort. Nowhere in this mythology is Asherah the consort of Baal. She is never associated with him. The same can be said for the epigraphic evidence of the first millennium. Tannit (probably Asherah) is the consort of Baal Ḥamon (El) consistently. Therefore, the Iron Age Canaanite evidence which we have examined tends on the whole to lend support to our thesis that the pairing of Baal and Asherah in the Hebrew Bible is an example of deuteronomistic polemic, and not a reflection of historical developments in Canaanite religion. On the other hand, the pairing of Baal and Aštart does reflect attested forms of Iron Age Canaanite religion accurately. In light of this evidence, the arguments of scholars who see Asherah becoming the consort of Baal at the end of the second millennium cannot be accepted. Such radical change in the associations of the Canaanite gods and goddesses is nowhere evident in extant texts. Though the epithets and some characteristics of deities were fluid, Canaanite religion was on the whole a conservative phenomenon.

---

l'Afrique du nord (Paris: Hachette, 1920; reprinted Osnabrück: Zeller, 1972) 4:259-60, 61-63. Gsell notes that Tannit and Aštart were both identified with Hera and Juno, and both called *Caelestis* in the west. On Tannit as Juno, see Hvidberg-Hansen, *La déesse Tnt* 119-20. Hvidberg-Hansen compares Tannit's iconography to that of Aphrodite Ourania at Cyprus.

Chapter 4

BAAL ŠAMÊM AND BAAL ADDĪR

Can we be reasonably certain that the "Baal" of the Hebrew Bible, with whom Asherah is associated in the Deuteronomistic History, is the storm god Hadad? As we have observed, in the religion of the first millennium, the epithet *ba'l* can be applied to a number of gods, just as *rbt*, "lady," is applied to various goddesses. In the Hebrew Bible, the plural usage "baals" (*bĕ'ālîm*) is attested for foreign gods generally understood. Yet the question is not insignificant for our thesis. If the "Baal" of the Bible is El rather than Hadad, the deuteronomistic association of Asherah and "Baal" would not be polemical at all; rather, it would be an accurate reflection of Canaanite religion. Most scholars, however, believe that the Baal of the Hebrew Bible is usually if not always the storm god Hadad (see the imagery of 1 Kgs 18:26, 27, 41-46). Because the somewhat elusive Baal Šamêm appears to be the Baal Carmel, it is important that we establish his identity as securely as possible. A second century inscription from Carmel on a statue of Zeus Heliopolis identifies the Baal of Baalbeq as the "god of Carmel." This Zeus Heliopolis has both solar and storm characteristics like Nabatean Zeus Helios, who is identified with Baal Šamêm. Thus, Baal Šamêm appears to be the Baal of Carmel.[1] We know from Sanchuniathon that Baal Šamêm (*Beelsamēn*) was considered a storm god associated with the sun in the heavens, and equated with Zeus (*PE* 1.10.7). Therefore, the evidence is consistent.

R. Oden, in a recent article, argued that Baal Šamêm is to be identified with El.[2] The best points made in favor of this thesis are these: (1) Oden notes the connection of Baal Šamêm with kings, often as their patron (as in Zakkur, *KAI* 202). (2) The Ha-

---

[1] Cross, "Notes on the Religion of Phoenicia in the Iron Age," (unpublished paper) argues that Baal Šamêm is a Hadad figure with solar features. He cites the above evidence and draws out its implications. Gsell (ibid. 4:295) argued that Baal Šamêm and Baal Ḥamon were two different gods. Eißfeldt ("Ba'alšamēm und Jahwe," *ZAW* 57 [1939] 1-30) provides an older review of the evidence. See also Albright, *Stone Age* 231, who identifies Baal Šamêm as a Hadad figure.

[2] "*Ba'al Šamēm* and *'Ēl*," *CBQ* 39 (1977) 457-73.

tra evidence is cited, where epithets normally associated with El are used of Baal Šamêm. He is called *qnh dy r*ᵎᵎ (for *'r*ᵎᵎ), "creator of the earth."[3] (3) Palmyrene Baal Šamêm is called *mr*ᵎ *'lm*ᵎ, "Lord of eternity," and *rḥmn*, "compassionate."[4] (4) Iluwer of Zakkur seems to be a Hadad figure, since Akkadian *wer/mer* generally is the equivalent of ᵈ*IM* elsewhere. Similarly, in the treaty of Esarhaddon and Baal of Tyre, both Baal Šamêm and Baal Ṣapon are mentioned, suggesting that Baal Šamêm and Hadad are not the same deity.[5]

There are, however, convincing explanations for all of these points, and much evidence that suggests that Baal Šamêm is Hadad. As we have argued in the case of the great goddesses, epithets, especially in the late first millennium, are a fluid category. We are, therefore, not particularly impressed by Baal Šamêm's epithets at Hatra or Palmyra. The association of Baal Šamêm with kings does not suggest El more than Baal-Hadad. The storm god is, after all, the king par excellence (see Sanchuniathon, *PE* 1.10.31). The presence of Iluwer, likely a Hadad figure, alongside Baal Šamêm in Zakkur, and the presence of Baal Ṣapon alongside Baal Šamêm in the treaty of Esarhaddon, do not necessarily suggest that Baal Šamêm is El, or even that he is not a Hadad figure. In the case of the treaty, local gods like Melqart and Ešmun are mentioned, and there is no reason why Baal Ṣapon and Baal Šamêm should not be seen also as local manifestations of Hadad, the latter with distinct solar characteristics absent from the former. The case of Iluwer and Baal Šamêm can be explained similarly. After all, there is much evidence for local manifestations of a single deity in West Semitic religion.

The evidence against Oden's thesis, and the data that favor the view that Baal Šamêm is a solarized form of Hadad, are significant. (1) A curse in the Karatepe inscription (*KAI* 26) invokes Baal Šamêm, and El *qōnē 'arṣ* and Šamaš '*ōlam* and the whole generation of the gods. Each is separated by a conjunctive *waw*. In no way can El *qōnē 'arṣ* and Šamaš '*ōlam* be seen as epithets of Baal Šamêm in this context. They are certainly separate dei-

---

³ Ibid. 467.

⁴ Ibid. 468-69.

⁵ R. Borger, *Die Inschriften Asarhaddons Königs von Assyrien* (AfO Beiheft 9; Graz: Weidner, 1956), 107-109. According to Borger, the treaty lists Bethel and Anatbethel, Baal Šamêm, Baal Malagê (?), Baal Ṣapon, Melqart, Ešmun, and Aštart. The readings Bethel and Anatbethel have been challenged. The treaty is discussed by M.L. Barré, *The God-List in the Treaty between Hannibal and Philip V of Macedonia* (Baltimore: Johns Hopkins University, 1983) 20, 111.

ties.[6] (2) The Adon Letter (*KAI* 266) reads at one point, . . . *šmy' w'rq' wb'lšmyn*. It seems evident that [**'ēl qōnēh*] ought to be reconstructed before *šmy' w'rq'*. This is, after all, one of El's traditional titles. It cannot be a title of Baal Šamêm in this context since a *waw* precedes his name.[7] Here we have more strong evidence that El and Baal Šamêm are separate deities. (3) The god list in *KAI* 78 reads *l'dn lb'l šmm wlrbt ltnt pn b'l wl'dn lb'l ḥmn wl'dn lb'l mgnm.* . . . This text, against Oden, distinguishes Baal Šamêm clearly from Baal Ḥamon, who is El.[8] (4) There is a further consideration. Oden argues that the position of primacy that Baal Šamêm takes in a number of inscriptions suggests that he is El, in light of El's primary place in the pantheon.[9] When we consider first millennium god lists, this argument becomes quite problematic. In Kilamuwa (*KAI* 24), Hadad (Baal Ṣimd) precedes El (Baal Ḥamon), as he does in Hadad (*KAI* 214), Panammu (*KAI* 215), and in the Punic dedication in *KAI* 78. In many instances in first millennium inscriptions, El is not at the head of the pantheon. If anything, this evidence suggests the opposite of Oden's thesis—that Baal Šamêm is Hadad![10]

We can establish with some confidence the identity of Baal Šamêm, but what of Baal Addīr? Baal Addīr occur frequently in Punic materials, and from time to time in Phoenician inscriptions. But who is Baal Addīr? The epithet *'addīr* and its feminine form *'adderet* (< **'addart*/*'addirt*) are used of a number of deities in the West Semitic world of the first millennium. It is used of Yahweh in the Hebrew Bible, of Aštart (*CIS* 1.255.4; 4842.7; 4843.4), of Tannit (El Hofra 132.1; *Sef* 15.49.3), of Melqart (the PN *'drmlqrt*).[11] We must attempt to identify Baal Addīr because he is paired with Tannit frequently in the series

---

[6] Against Oden, "*Ba'al Šamêm*," 462.

[7] Against Oden, ibid. 465.

[8] Ibid. 466. Baal Šamêm was worshiped at Carthage. He is mentioned in a dedication in *CIS* 1.379. Compare this to the thousands of dedications to Baal Ḥamon and Tannit.

[9] Ibid. 470.

[10] More evidence for the identification of Baal Šamêm as a Hadad figure is listed by Cross, "Religion of Phoenicia." He notes that Macrobius, Saturnalia 1.23.10 identifies Adad and Baal Šamêm explicitly. In addition, we note that at Palmyra, Baal Ḥamon and Baal Šamêm are distinguished, suggesting again that Baal Šamêm is not El.

[11] Benz, *Personal Names* 262. The form with *ayin* should not be regarded as problematic. Punic and Neo-Punic inscriptions are often characterized by such aberrant spellings. See the name *'drb'l*, spelled often *'drb'l*. J.M. Sola Solé, "Inscripciones Fenicias de la Península Ibérica," *Sefarad* 15 (1955) 49, no. 5 pairs *tnt 'dr* and *b'l 'dr*.

of inscriptions from el Hofra.[12] Is Baal Addīr yet another epithet of El, who is usually called Baal Ḥamon in the Punic world? Or is it perhaps an epithet of Baal-Hadad? The answer to this question is central to our thesis, for if Baal Addīr can be shown to be Baal-Hadad, then we cannot assert that Asherah (likely Tannit in the Punic west) and Baal-Hadad are never paired in the extant evidence of Canaanite religion. On the other hand, if Baal Addīr can be shown to be yet another epithet of El, our evidence remains consistent, and we can assert with confidence that Asherah and Baal-Hadad are never paired as consorts in Canaanite religion of the second millennium and first millennium BCE.

The el Hofra inscriptions present us with evidence that Baal Addīr was paired with Tannit in areas of the Punic world. El Hofra 4.1 reads *l'dn lb'l 'dr wlrb'tn tnt p'n' b'l*, "To the lord, to Baal Addīr, and to our lady, Tannit the face of Baal. . . ." Similar dedications mentioning Baal Addīr and Tannit together are to be found in 12.1-2; 13.1-2; 16.1; 17.1-2; 19.1-2. Inscription 21 reads *lb'l ltnt p'n' b'l*, Baal appearing here presumably as a shortened form of Baal Addīr. There are numerous other inscriptions in the el Hofra corpus that mention Baal Addīr (over twenty in all). These can be compared profitably to other Punic and Neo-Punic dedications to Baal Ḥamon and Tannit, many of which we have discussed previously. Yet in the el Hofra corpus itself, we find a dedication to Baal Ḥamon and Tannit (24.1). What are we to make of this? In el Hofra 27.2, a temple (*bt*) of Baal Addīr is mentioned. The sign of Tannit as well as the characteristic disk and crescent appear on most of the above-mentioned stelae of Baal Addīr or Baal Addīr and Tannit.[13] A consort relationship between the two is implied by this evidence, as well as the conclusion that Baal Addīr is El. In inscription 42.1 a *mlk* offering is dedicated to Baal Addīr: *l'dn lb'l 'dr ndr hn'. . .mlk šm' ql'*. The similarity in both form and content to the typical, ubiquitous *mlk* dedication to Baal Ḥamon is obvious, only the type of *mlk* offering is not specified.

A consideration of the el Hofra evidence suggests strongly

---

[12] On the el Hofra materials, see A. Berthier and R. Charlier, *'El Hofra* (2 vols.; Paris: Arts et métiers graphiques, 1955).

[13] See ibid., volume of plates, nos. 20a, 22c, and 25b, for Tannit's sign with palms and/or the caduceus, as well as the disk and crescent, suggesting Baal Addīr is Baal Ḥamon. On the disk and crescent as archaic symbols of El in Byblos and elsewhere, see R. du Mesnil du Buisson, *Nouvelles études* 73-74, and Cross, *Canaanite Myth* 35-36. We do not accept du Mesnil's identification of Baal Addīr as Kôthar. Gsell, *Histoire* 4:296, suggested the possibility that Baal Addīr was in fact Baal Ḥamon, but was inclined to think not.

that Baal Addīr is an alternative epithet of El in the Punic sphere of the late first millennium, found alongside the more popular epithet Baal Ḥamon. The epithet Baal Addīr appears to have been particularly popular in the area of el Hofra. Not only is Baal Addīr paired with Tannit in the manner of Baal Ḥamon, but Baal Addīr is also offered a *mlk* sacrifice, a phenomenon characteristic of El/Baal Ḥamon's cult in the west, and never associated with the cult of Baal Šamêm in the west. The disk and crescent, characteristic symbols of El/Baal Ḥamon, appear frequently on the Baal Addīr stelae. Baal Addīr and Baal Ḥamon are never mentioned in the same inscription. If we are correct and Baal Addīr is Baal Ḥamon, then Baal Addīr is El, and Tannit is his expected consort.

The Greek inscriptions from el Hofra lend weight to our argument. Here Kronos and *thenneith phenē bal* (=*tannit panê ba'l*) appear together. Kronos is equated with El in Sanchuniathon and elsewhere. At el Hofra, Kronos seems to substitute for Baal Addīr. The el Hofra Latins suggest the same relationship. Vows are presented to Saturn, who elsewhere is equated with El.

Does the rest of the extant evidence concerning Baal Addīr from Phoenician and Punic inscriptions support our thesis? In general, it does. Nowhere in the epigraphic corpus do Baal Addīr and Baal Ḥamon occur side by side in the same inscription. If this were the case, it could imply that they were different deities. In the inscription of Šipṭiba'l of Byblos (*KAI* 9 B 5), dated to ca. 500 BCE, we find the following reading in a fragmentary context: *[. . .]m wb'l 'd[r. . .] b'lt wkl '[lnm. . .]*. Dunand, Février and others have adopted the restoration [**ba'l šam]êm* before *ba'l 'add[īr]*,[14] on the basis of the presence of the letter *mem* after the break. Though appealing for the purposes of our reconstruction, we must emphasize that this can only be taken as a possibility, though it is a likely one. In such a pantheon list, we would expect the name of a prominent deity, and the name would have to end in *mem*. The name could not be another epithet for Baal Addīr, since his name is preceded by the conjunction *waw*. There are few candidates for the restoration other than Baal Šamêm. If this restoration is correct, then Baal Addīr and Baal Šamêm (Hadad) are clearly distinguished.

In a series of Latin inscriptions from the western Mediterranean, Baal Addīr occurs with various epithets: *deo patrio Baliddir augustus* (*CIL* 8.19121, 19122); *deo sancto Baliddir* (19123).

---

[14] J.G. Février, "A Propos de Ba'al Addir," *Sem* 2 (1949) 21-28, who cites Dunand.

The expression *deo patrio* is of interest, since it seems to reflect the West Semitic epithet *'ab*, "father," one of the best attested epithets of El. In addition, *augustus* may reflect the West Semitic El epithet *'elyōn*, "the most high." These are additional points in favor of the identification of Baal Addīr and El.

Finally, there is a single text where Baal Addīr and Baal Hamon seem to be equated. In *KAI* 162.1, from second-century Constantine, *b'l hmn bl 'dr* occurs,[15] with no *waw* conjunction separating the two names. The lack of the conjunction strongly suggests an accumulation of epithets for a single deity here. The most desirable translation would be "Baal Hamon, the majestic lord. . . ." Compare *CIS* 1.4943, *l'l lb'l hmn*, "To El, to the lord of Hamon,"[16] with no *waw* separating the name and the following epithet. Clearly, a single deity is the subject of each dedication.

There are a number of occurrences of a divine name that combines the elements *mlk* (**milk*, "king")[17] and *'dr*, and these ought to be discussed in light of our thesis. On coins from Phoenicia proper and from its western colonies, the divine title *'drmlk* (**'addīrmilk*, "the majestic king") occurs. This is also attested as a personal name (see *CIS* 1.1929.4). Is this Addīrmilk the god Baal Addīr? This seems likely for a number of reasons.

A variant of this epithet is most probably to be found in Plutarch's *Isis and Osiris* 357, where the transparently West Semitic *malkandros* ought to be reconstructed **milk'addīr*.[18] The confusion between West Semitic *'addīr* and Greek *andros* needs little explanation. The two words sound very similar. This Malkandros, or **milk'addīr*, is described very much like El. Not only is he the king of Byblos (El's special city according to Sanchuniathon)[19] but he is also the husband of Astarte, and there is a version of a child sacrifice myth found here. According to

[15] Spellings like *bl* and *'dr* for older *b'l* and *'dr* are common in Neo-Punic texts.

[16] For discussion of the vocalization and identification of *hmn*, see Cross, *Canaanite Myth* 26-28.

[17] **milk* is the preferred Phoenician vocalization of this period, though historical considerations suggest **malk* for Biblical Hebrew.

[18] This has been suggested by a number of past commentators. See for example Friedrich-Röllig, *Phönizisch-Punische Grammatik* par.58c n.2, as well as du Mesnil, *Nouvelles études* 61, and recently, J. Ebach and U. Rüterswörden, "ADRMLK, 'Moloch' und BA'AL ADR," *UF* 11 (1979) 224. This correspondence is widely accepted in scholarly circles. Against Weinfeld, "The Worship of Moloch," 137-38, who reconstructs *mlk 'dm* here!

[19] *PE* 1.10.20, 35, *kai polin prōtēn ktizei tēn epi phoinikēs Byblon*. We are told later that Kronos gave Byblos, the first city, to Dione/Baaltis (=**ba'lat*, "the lady").

this story, Isis, who nursed the son of the king and queen, burned the child at night, turned into a swallow, and flew around a pillar lamenting. This is to be compared to the multiforms of the myth of El's sacrifice of his own son in Sanchuniathon (*PE* 1.10.33-34, 44). Kronos/El, dressing his son in royal attire, sacrificed him at a time of crisis. From Diodorus we know human sacrifices to El/Kronos occurred at night. Diodorus also relates the myth of El sacrificing his own children. The solution we propose is this: the Plutarch myth is another multiform of the myth preserved in Sanchuniathon and in Diodorus, and the king Malkandros is none other than El/Kronos. In the Plutarch version of the myth, it is Isis, and not El himself, who performs the sacrifice of El's child. Thus we assert the equation El/Kronos = Baal Addīr = Milkaddīr/Addīrmilk. The deity *'adrammelek* of 2 Kgs 17:31 (Bab. *'adarmelek*), who takes human sacrifices, is best understood in light of this evidence. We should reconstruct the name ***'addīrmelek*, on the basis of the consonantal text, the Babylonian vocalization, and what we know about Milkaddīr from other texts. Thus we reject the popular proposal to emend 2 Kgs 17:31 to Adadmelek.[20]

The title "king" (*milk*/*malk*) makes perfect sense for El, who possesses it in numerous texts of both the second and first millennium BCE.[21] Baal Addīr and Milkaddīr are likely archaic Byblian epithets for El, preserved mostly on the fringes of the Phoenician world by the late first millennium. The preservation of archaic epithets of deity on the fringes has been observed both in the case of Baal Ḥamon and for Tannit.[22] The tendency

---

[20] See A. Pohl, "Zu 4 Könige 17,31," *Bib* 22 (1941) 35, on Adad-milki in the Halaf inscriptions. This DN may occur in several personal names (e.g. ᵈAdad-milki-iddin), but see Kaufman below. Pohl argues that Adrammelek in 2 Kgs 17:31 is Adad-milki, positing an orthographic shift of $d > r$ in this text. See also R. de Vaux, *Studies in Old Testament Sacrifice* (Cardiff: University of Wales, 1964) 89 and the review of K. Deller, in *Or* 34 (1965) 382-83. There may be evidence of children sacrificed to Adad-milki at Halaf. Yet this does not validate what appears to be an unnecessary consonantal emendation of the text. See our discussion of the Canaanite cult of human sacrifice in notes 33 and 34, chapter 1. There is no convincing evidence that suggests Canaanite Baal took human sacrifices. Even the Halaf evidence has been questioned. See S. Kaufman, "The Enigmatic Adad-Milki," *JNES* 37 (1978) 101-110, who argues against Deller et al. that logographic Adad-Milki can be read differently.

[21] See such onomastic examples as *'ilu(AN)-milku* in *PRU* IV. El is portrayed as a king in *PE* 1.10.29, 36, 44, as well as in the Ugaritic texts. The Byblian onomasticon of the Iron Age contains many **milk* names, and these are often paralleled by biblical names with El. See for example *yhwmlk*//*yĕhîʾēl*, *'rmlk*//*'ûrîʾēl*. On *milk* as an El epithet, see M. Pope, *El in the Ugaritic Texts* 26.

[22] See notes 62 and 63, chapter 3, for references.

for archaic usages of various kinds to survive and even flourish on the fringes of a civilization is a widely attested phenomenon.

Chapter 5

CONCLUSION

Scholars have long pondered the removal of the bronze serpent Nehushtan from the Jerusalem temple by Hezekiah. It seems quite evident that Hezekiah's reform followed guidelines set up by the deuteronomistic school, who approved of his actions regarding Nehushtan (2 Kgs 18:4).[1] This cult object, the creation of which was traditionally ascribed to Moses in the wilderness period, did not lack respectable lineage. In fact the tradition of Mosaic provenance must have been very strong, for even the deuteronomistic narrators confirm it, but provide a justification for its removal from the temple (the people worshiped the object). It is noteworthy that the bronze serpent is removed at the same time as the Asherah.

Was there a relationship between the two cult objects destroyed by Hezekiah and opposed by the deuteronomistic school? There is a good chance that there was. In Canaanite religion of the Bronze and Iron Ages, the goddess Asherah appears to have had associations with the serpent. If we accept the likely identification of Tannit as Asherah and the etymology of *tannit* proposed by Cross (feminine of *tannīn* which would mean "the one of the serpent"), we would have evidence of this association. Further, Asherah appears to have carried a second epithet in the Bronze Age, *dāt batni*, also "the one of the serpent."[2] If we accept Albright's suggestion that Ugaritic *'aṭiratu yammi* ought to be understood as "She who treads on (the) sea (dragon)," we have more evidence for the somewhat obscure association of Asherah and the serpent.[3] One suspects

---

[1] See Weinfeld, *Deuteronomy* 163-64; "The Emergence of the Deuteronomic Movement: The Historical Antecedents," in *Das Deuteronomium. Entstehung, Gestalt und Botschaft*, ed. N. Lohfink (BETL 68; Leuven: Leuven University, 1985) 91; Lohfink, "Deuteronomy," *IDBSup* 231; Rosenbaum, "Hezekiah's Reform," 23-43.

[2] See n.63, chapter 3 for discussion as well as Cross, "The Origin and Early Evolution," 12* n.27 and Albright, "The Early Alphabetic Inscriptions from the Sinai and their Decipherment," *BASOR* 110 (1948) 6-22. In the proto-Sinaitic inscriptions, the epithet *dāt batni* parallels *tannit*.

[3] *Archaeology and the Religion of Israel* 77-78; *Yahweh and the Gods of Canaan*

that an early myth associating the serpent/sea dragon and Asherah has been lost. Perhaps a reflex of this myth is preserved in the Eden story in Genesis. After all, *ḥawwâ* (Eve) is an attested epithet of Tannit/Asherah in the first millennium BCE.[4] The frequent appearance of the serpent in representations of Qudšu (Asherah) from Bronze Age Egypt must also be taken into account here.[5] The cumulative evidence associating the serpent and the goddess Asherah suggests in our view that the bronze serpent Nehushtan of the Jerusalem temple may have been an Asherah cult symbol, and was therefore removed by Hezekiah along with the asherah itself. The symbol had been perfectly legitimate up to that time. It even had a prestigious pedigree.[6]

It has been suggested by others that Nehushtan was legitimate in the cultus before the development of the deuteronomistic ideology. However, we do not believe a case has been made for Nehushtan's association with the cult of Asherah. In any case, the bronze serpent, the asherah, and the pillar were opposed by the deuteronomistic school, though they were apparently legitimate outside such circles (Hosea, however, criticized the *maṣṣēbôt*; see Hos 3:4; 10:1, 2). Why were the members of the deuteronomistic school so concerned that these symbols be removed from Yahweh's cult? Nascent monotheism is unfortunately no solution. Deut 4:19-20 and 29:25 make this clear. There is no denial of the existence of other gods here, but rather the assertion that the worship of other deities was allotted to other nations, not Israel. Israel is Yahweh's ʿ*am naḥǎlâ*. We

---

105-106; Albright has been followed by Pope, "Aṯirat," 247 and Cross, *Canaanite Myth* 31.

[4] See *KAI* 89.1, *rbt ḥwt 'lt*, **rabbat ḥawwat 'ilat*, "The Lady Ḥawwah, Elat," who is likely Asherah/Elat/Tannit. Elat is a well known epithet of Asherah both in the Bronze and Iron Ages. "The Lady" (*rbt*) is used frequently of Tannit in the Punic world. For another Punic attestation of *ḥwt*, see M. Lidzbarski, *Ephemeris für semitische Epigraphik* (Gießen: Töpelmann, 1915) 3:285. For the epithet Elat in the Iron Age, see n.48, chapter 3. On the possibility of an old Asherah myth behind the Genesis Eden story, see H. Wallace, *The Eden Narrative* (HSM 32; Atlanta: Scholars, 1985) 158, who hesitates to take a firm position, but opts for the skeptical view. Wallace does not remark on the possible relationship of Nehushtan to Asherah's cultus.

[5] *ANEP* 471, 472(?), 474. Stela 473 shows Qudšu, El (Ptah) and Rešep, where Qudšu appears naked on a lion with lotus and serpents. This evidence is decisive. We know from Ugarit that Qudšu is an epithet of Canaanite Asherah. See Cross, *Canaanite Myth* 33-35.

[6] Weinfeld ("Emergence of the Deuteronomic Movement," 85) argues that Nehushtan was smashed because of the influence of an "iconoclastic tendency" from Israel making itself felt in Judah. Weinfeld refers to the asherah (as well as pillars and high places) as "pagan elements" in the cult.

have a highly developed covenantal ideology of Yahweh's exclusive suzerainty here, but not monotheism.[7] Monolatry or henotheism better describe the deuteronomistic ideology.[8] Elsewhere in Deuteronomy, covenant language predominates, as many have pointed out.[9] The deuteronomistic ideology is

[7] Against A. Rofé, "The Covenant in the Land of Moab," in *Das Deuteronomium* 319, who argues that Deuteronomy is a "monotheistic work." Rofé does however recognize that the demands of a covenant with Yahweh do not in themselves include implicitly the denial of the existence of other deities, only that other deities cannot be worshiped.

On the date and provenance of Deut 4:1-40 and 29:21-27, see the discussions of Lohfink, "Auslegung deuteronomistischer Texte, IV," *Bib Leb* 5 (1964) 250-53; J. Levenson, "Who Inserted the Book of the Torah?" *HTR* 68 (1975) 203-33, esp. 215 and 221 n.38; R.E. Friedman, *The Exile and Biblical Narrative* (HSM 22; Chico, CA: Scholars, 1981) 17-18. Lohfink and Levenson see Deut 4:1-40 as a unit and assign an exilic date; Friedman argues an exilic date for vv 25-31. All agree on an exilic date for 29:21-27. The close relationship between 4:19 and 29:25 is discussed by Levenson, who notes that both passages build on Deut 32:8-9, which he assumes is "ancient" (215).

The date of Deuteronomy 32 has been widely debated. In its present form, sections of the song have very close affinities to exilic and post-exilic literature, particularly to the work of Second Isaiah and the school of Second Isaiah. There are however numerous archaisms present in the poem which some scholars have taken to indicate an early date (11th c.: Eißfeldt, *Das Lied Moses Deuteronomium 32, 1-43 und das Lehrgedicht Asaphs Psalm 78 samt einer Analyse der Umgebung des Mose-Liedes* [Berichte über die Verhandlungen der Sächsischen Akademie der Wissenschaft zu Leipzig, Philologisch-historisch Klasse 104.5; Berlin: Akademie, 1958] and Albright, *Yahweh and the Gods of Canaan* 17 and "Some Remarks on the Song of Moses in Deuteronomy xxxii," *VT* 9 [1959] 339-46). Others have settled for a date in the period of the divided kingdoms (G.E. Wright, "The Lawsuit of God: A Form-Critical Study of Deuteronomy 32," in *Israel's Prophetic Heritage*, ed. B. Anderson and W. Harrelson [New York: Harper, 1962] 40; D.N. Freedman, "Divine Names and Titles in Early Hebrew Poetry," in *Magnalia Dei. Essays in Memory of George Ernest Wright*, ed. F.M. Cross, et al. [Garden City: Doubleday, 1976] 57, 77-80 and bibliography on 101 n.60; Cross, *Canaanite Myth* 264). Yet the most convincing view is that a poem with archaic features was reworked during the exile. J. Luyten, "Primeval and Eschatological Overtones in the Song of Moses (Dt 32, 1-43)," in *Das Deuteronomium* 341-47, presents the evidence for an exilic date, as did the earlier treatments of von Rad, *Deuteronomy* (Old Testament Library; Philadelphia: Westminster, 1966) 195-200 and A.D.H. Mayes, *Deuteronomy* (New Century Bible; London: Oliphants, 1979) 380-82. D.A. Robertson, *Linguistic Evidence in Dating Early Hebrew Poetry* (SBLDS 3; Missoula, MT: Society of Biblical Literature, 1972) 155 considers vv 8-20 early. The monotheistic statements of vv 39-42 are in tension with the statements in vv 8-9.

[8] B. Halpern, in a future monograph, will discuss the emergence of radical monotheism in Israel. See provisionally " 'Brisker Pipes than Poetry': The Development of Israelite Monotheism," in *Judaic Perspectives on Ancient Israel*, J. Neusner et al. eds. (Philadelphia: Fortress, 1987) 77-115.

[9] There is much literature on the covenantal aspects of Deuteronomy. On the covenantal background of the language of love, see W.L. Moran, "The Ancient Near Eastern Background of the Love of God in Deuteronomy," *CBQ* 25 (1963) 77-

perhaps the result of a logical extension of Yahweh's exclusive claim on Israel, his ʿ*am naḥălâ*.[10]

The deuteronomistic school appears to have been profoundly influenced by the thought of Hosea, who criticized *bāmôt*, *maṣṣēbôt*, the bull icons of Bethel and the worship of Baal. The rejection of the asherah was, however, a deuteronomistic innovation. Nowhere in Hosea is the asherah condemned. In fact, before the reforming kings in Judah, the asherah seems to have been entirely legitimate. The deuteronomistic school were innovators, and not conservatives attempting to purge the cult of Yahweh of "foreign" or "pagan" elements. It is quite clear that scholars can no longer write in this manner about the cult of Yahweh in the monarchic period; we can no longer accept uncritically the ideology of the deuteronomists themselves. A thorough analysis of the evidence suggests a different model for understanding monarchic Yahwism: Otherwise legitimate Yahwistic symbols and practices (the bull icons of Dan and Bethel, the *bāmôt*, the asherah, Nehushtan, the *maṣṣēbôt*) are judged illegitimate by the deuteronomistic school, who make use of polemical distortion as a technique to eliminate these practices and remove these symbols from the cultus. In the case of the asherah, the deuteronomists associate it with the cult of Baal. Extra-biblical evidence, in contrast, suggests both that the asherah was a legitimate symbol in Yahweh's cult, and that the goddess Asherah was never associated intimately with Baal in Canaanite religion.[11]

---

87. For other discussions of covenant in Deuteronomy, see Lohfink, "Dt. 26, 17-19 und die 'Bundesformel,'" *ZKT* 91 (1969) 517-53; Weinfeld, "Emergence of the Deuteronomic Movement," 79-81; Rofé, ibid. 310-20.

[10] Weinfeld argues that an "iconoclastic tendency" from Israel "pervaded Judah after the destruction of Samaria." He feels this was responsible for the smashing of Nehushtan and the removal of the asherahs, pillars and high places in Hezekiah's reform (ibid., 85). Unfortunately, this theory does not adequately explain the removal of the high places, which Weinfeld argues were Canaanite cult sites possessing pillars and wooden symbols. There is more than enough evidence that these sanctuaries were Yahwistic, as were the hated rival sanctuaries of Bethel and Dan. See chapter 1, n.44 on Arad. Archeological evidence suggests that sacrifices at Arad ceased in the time of Hezekiah, but that the temple there finally ceased to exist only in the time of Josiah. Weinfeld's theory also does not account for the presumed acceptability of the cherubim and other cultic symbols and images in the Jerusalem temple; the reforming kings did nothing to remove these.

[11] J. Tigay's recent discussion of the Kuntillet Ajrûd evidence illustrates well the traditional scholarly viewpoint. Tigay minimizes the importance of the data from Kuntillet Ajrûd, arguing that "the references to YHWH and an *asherah* show at most the heterodoxy of one or more Yahwists at a distant site apparently frequented by others in addition to Israelites" (*No Other Gods* 29).

A place for Asherah and her cult symbol in Israelite religion seems assured by recent discoveries and research on other extant texts. We believe that in the future more scholars will adopt the view that Asherah had some role in the cult of Yahweh. Asherah and her cult symbol were legitimate not only in popular Yahwism, but in the official cult as well. The evidence of the Hebrew Bible alone suggests strongly that Asherah and the asherah were considered legitimate in the state cult, both of the north and the south, in Jerusalem, Samaria and Bethel, and probably in very conservative circles. The prohibitions and polemics against Asherah and her cult symbol attest to their popularity in the cult of Yahweh in Iron Age Israel; the evidence from Kuntillet Ajrûd (and probably Khirbet el-Qôm) confirms this. An examination of Canaanite sources adds comparative depth and weight to any analysis of this data. Since Asherah remains El's consort and is not associated with Baal in Iron Age Canaanite religion, we can assert more confidently that Asherah's association with Baal in the Deuteronomistic History is polemical rather than a reflection of historical developments in West Semitic religion. Such polemic is to be compared to the deuteronomistic attack on the bulls of the northern sanctuaries and on the cult of human sacrifice. The stamp of Yahwistic illegitimacy is accorded to Asherah and her cult symbol when they are associated with Baal and his cultus.

BIBLIOGRAPHY

Aharoni, Y. "Arad: Its Inscriptions and Temple." *BA* 31 (1968) 2-32.

Ahlström, G.W. *Aspects of Syncretism in Israelite Religion.* Lund: Gleerup, 1963.

————. *Royal Administration and National Religion in Ancient Palestine.* Leiden: Brill, 1982.

Albright, W.F. "The Evolution of the West-Semitic Divinity ʿAn- ʿAnat- ʿAttâ." *AJSL* 41 (1925) 73-101, 283-85.

————. *Archaeology and the Religion of Israel.* Baltimore: Johns Hopkins University, 1942.

————. "A Prince of Taanach in the Fifteenth Century B.C." *BASOR* 94 (1944) 12-27.

————. "The Early Alphabetic Inscriptions from the Sinai and their Decipherment." *BASOR* 110 (1948) 6-22.

————. *From Stone Age to Christianity.* Garden City: Doubleday, 1957.

————. "Some Remarks on the Song of Moses in Deuteronomy xxxii." *VT* 9 (1959) 339-46.

————. *Yahweh and the Gods of Canaan.* Garden City: Doubleday, 1968.

Alt, A. "Der Stadtstaat Samaria." *Kleine Schriften zur Geschichte des Volkes Israel.* 3 vols. Munich: Becksche, 1953. 3:258-302.

————. "Die Heimat des Deuteronomiums." *Kleine Schriften.* 2:250-75.

————. "The Monarchy in the Kingdom of Israel and Judah." In *Essays on Old Testament History and Religion*, trans. R.A. Wilson 241-59. Oxford: Blackwell, 1966.

Amsler, S., Jacob, E., and Keller, C.A. *Osée, Joël, Abdias, Jonas, Amos*. CAT 11a. Neuchâtel: Delachaux & Niestlé, 1965.

Andersen, F. and Freedman, D.N. *Hosea*. AB 24. Garden City: Doubleday, 1980.

Angerstorfer, A. "Asherah als 'consort of Jahwe' oder Ashirtah?" *Biblische Notizen* 17 (1982) 7-16.

Astour, M.C. "Ya'udi." *IDBSup* 975.

Attridge, H. and Oden, R., eds. *De Dea Syria*. SBLTT 9. Missoula, MT: Scholars, 1976.

――――. *Philo of Byblos. The Phoenician History*. CBQMS 9. Washington: Catholic Biblical Association, 1981.

Barr, J. "Philo of Byblos and his 'Phoenician History.'" *BJRL* 57 (1974) 17-68.

Barré, M.L. *The God-List in the Treaty between Hannibal and Philip V of Macedonia*. Baltimore: Johns Hopkins University, 1983.

Baumgarten, A.I. *The Phoenician History of Philo of Byblos. A Commentary*. Etudes préliminaires aux religions orientales dans l'Empire romain 89. Leiden: Brill, 1981.

Beck, P. "The Drawings from Horvat Teiman (Kuntillet 'Ajrûd)." *Tel Aviv* 9 (1982) 3-86.

Benigni, G. "Il 'segno di Tanit' in Oriente." *Revista di studi fenici* 3 (1975) 17-18.

Benz, F.L. *Personal Names in the Phoenician and Punic Inscriptions*. Studia Pohl 8. Rome: Pontifical Biblical Institute, 1972.

Bernhardt, K.-H. "Aschera in Ugarit und im Alten Testament." *Mitteilungen des Instituts für Orientforschung* 13 (1967) 163-74.

Berthier, A. and Charlier, R. *'El Hofra*. 2 vols. Paris: Arts et métiers graphiques, 1955.

Betlyon, J.W. "The Cult of 'Asherah/'Ēlat at Sidon." *JNES* 44 (1985) 53-56.

Bisi, A.M. *Le stele puniche*. Studi Semitici 27. Rome: Istituto di studi del vicino Oriente, 1967.

Blenkinsopp, J. *A History of Prophecy in Israel.* Philadelphia: Westminster, 1983.

Bonello, V., et al. *Missione archeologica italiana a Malta.* 8 vols. Rome: University of Rome, 1964-73.

Bordreuil, P. "Attestations inédites de Melqart, Baal Ḥamon et Baal Ṣaphon à Tyr." *Studia Phoenicia IV.* Namur: Société des études classiques, 1986. 77-86.

Borger, R. *Die Inschriften Asarhaddons Königs von Assyrien.* AfO Beiheft 9. Graz: Weidner, 1956.

Botterweck, G.J. and Ringgren, H., eds. *Theological Dictionary of the Old Testament.* Trans. J.T. Willis. 4 vols. (thus far). Grand Rapids: Eerdmans, 1974-.

Bright, J. "The Date of the Prose Sermons of Jeremiah." *JBL* 70 (1951) 15-35.

―――. *Jeremiah.* AB 21. Garden City: Doubleday, 1965.

Brueggeman, W. "Isaiah 55 and Deuteronomic Theology." *ZAW* 80 (1968) 191-203.

Buccellati, G. *Cities and Nations of Ancient Syria.* Studi Semitici 26. Rome: University of Rome, 1967.

Caquot, A. "La tablette *RS* 24.252. Et la question des Rephaïm ougaritiques." *Syria* 53 (1976) 295-304.

Cassuto, U. *The Goddess Anath.* English ed. Jerusalem: Magnes, 1971.

Childs, B. *The Book of Exodus: A Critical, Theological Commentary.* Old Testament Library. Philadelphia: Westminster, 1974.

Collon, D. *The Seal Impressions from Tell Atchana/Alalakh.* AOAT 27. Neukirchen-Vluyn: Neukirchener and Kevelaer: Butzon & Bercker, 1975.

Corpus Inscriptionum Latinarum: Consilio et Auctoritate Academiae Litterarum Regiae Borussicae editum. Berlin: Reimer, 1863-.

Corpus Inscriptionum Semiticarum: Ab Academia Inscriptionum et Litterarum Humaniorum conditum atque digestum. Paris: e Reipublicae typographeo, 1881-.

Couroyer, B. *"BRK* et les formules égyptiennes de salutation." *RB* 85 (1978) 575-85.

Cowley, A. *Aramaic Papyri of the Fifth Century B.C.* Oxford: Clarendon, 1923.

Cross, F.M. and Freedman, D.N. *Early Hebrew Orthography.* AOS 36. New Haven: American Oriental Society, 1952.

Cross, F.M. "Yahweh and the God of the Patriarchs." *HTR* 55 (1962) 225-59.

――――. "The Origin and Early Evolution of the Alphabet." *Eretz Israel* 8 (1967) 8*-24.*

――――. *Canaanite Myth and Hebrew Epic.* Cambridge: Harvard University, 1973.

――――. "A Reconstruction of the Judean Restoration." *Int* 29 (1975) 187-202 = *JBL* 94 (1975) 4-18.

――――. "Notes on the Religion of Phoenicia in the Iron Age," Unpublished paper.

Day, J. "A Case of Inner Scriptural Interpretation." *JTS* 31 (1980) 309-19.

――――. "Asherah in the Hebrew Bible and Northwest Semitic Literature." *JBL* 105 (1986) 385-408.

Deller, K. Review of R. de Vaux, *Studies in Old Testament Sacrifice.* *Or* 34 (1965) 382-86.

Dever, W. "Iron Age Epigraphic Material from the Area of Khirbet el-Kôm." *HUCA* 40/41 (1970) 139-204.

――――. "Recent Archaeological Confirmation of the Cult of Asherah in Ancient Israel." *Hebrew Studies* 23 (1982) 37-44.

――――. "Material Remains and the Cult in Ancient Israel: An Essay in Archaeological Systematics." In *The Word of the Lord Shall Go Forth: Essays in Honor of David Noel Freedman in Celebration of His Sixtieth Birthday,* 571-87. C.L. Meyers and M. O'Connor, ed. Winona Lake, IN: Eisenbrauns, 1983.

――――. "Asherah, Consort of Yahweh? New Evidence from Kuntillet ʿAjrûd." *BASOR* 255 (1984) 21-37.

Dion, P. *La langue de Ya'udi.* Waterloo, ONT: CPASRC, 1974.

Diringer, D. *Le iscrizioni antico-ebraiche palestinesi.* Firenze: Monnier, 1934.

Donner, H. and Röllig, W. *Kanaanäische und aramäische Inschriften.* 4th ed. 3 vols. Wiesbaden: Harrassowitz, 1979.

Donner, H. *Herrschergestalten in Israel.* Verständliche Wissenschaft 103. Berlin, Heidelberg and New York: Springer, 1970.

———. "The Separate States of Israel and Judah." In *Israelite and Judaean History*, 381-434. J.H. Hayes and J.M. Miller, ed. Old Testament Library. Philadelphia: Westminster, 1977.

Dothan, M. "A Phoenician Inscription from ʿAkko." *IEJ* 35 (1985) 81-94 and pl. 13A and B.

———. "The Phoenician Inscription from ʿAkko." *Eretz Israel* 18 (1985) 116-23 (Hebrew).

Driver, G.R. "Reflections on Recent Articles." *JBL* 73 (1954) 125-36.

Dupont-Sommer, A. "Une stèle araméenne d'un prêtre de Baʿal trouvée en Egypte." *Syria* 33 (1956) 79-87.

Ebach, J. and Rüterswörden, U. "ADRMLK, 'Moloch' und BAʿAL ADR." *UF* 11 (1979) 219-26.

Edwards, I.E.S. "A Relief of Qudshu—Astarte—Anath in the Winchester College Collection." *JNES* 14 (1955) 49-51.

Eißfeldt, O. *Molk als Opferbegriff im Punischen und Hebräischen und das Ende des Gottes Moloch.* Halle: Niemeyer, 1935.

———. "Baʿalšamēm und Jahwe." *ZAW* 57 (1939) 1-30.

———. "Lade und Stierbild." *ZAW* 58 (1940/41) 190-215.

———. *El im ugaritischen Pantheon.* Berlin: Akademie, 1951.

———. *Sanchunjaton von Berut und Ilumilku von Ugarit.* Beiträge zur Religionsgeschichte des Altertums 5. Halle: Niemeyer, 1952.

———. *Das Lied Moses Deuteronomium 32, 1-43 und das Lehrgedicht Asaphs Psalm 78 samt einer Analyse der Umgebung des Mose-Liedes.* Berichte über die Verhandlungen der Sächsischen Akademie der Wissenschaften zu

Leipzig, Philologisch-historische Klasse, 104.5. Berlin: Akademie, 1958.

Emerton, J.A. "New Light on Israelite Religion: The Implications of the Inscriptions from Kuntillet ʿAjrud." *ZAW* 94 (1982) 2-20.

Engle, J.R. "Pillar Figurines of Iron Age Israel and Asherah-Asherim." Ph.D. dissertation, University of Pittsburgh, 1979.

Février, J.G. "A propos de Baʿal Addir." *Sem* 2 (1949) 21-28.

Fitzmyer, J. "The Phoenician Inscription from Pyrgi." *JAOS* 86 (1966) 285-97.

———. *The Aramaic Inscriptions of Sefîre.* BibOr 19. Rome: Pontifical Biblical Institute, 1967.

Fohrer, G. "Umkehr und Erlösung beim Propheten Hosea." *TZ* 11 (1955) 161-85.

———. "Die Aufbau der Apokalypse des Jesajabuchs (Is. 24-27)." *CBQ* 25 (1963) 34-45.

Freedman, D.N. "The Chronicler's Purpose." *CBQ* 23 (1961) 436-42.

———. "Divine Names and Titles in Early Hebrew Poetry." In *Magnalia Dei. Essays in Memory of George Ernest Wright,* ed. F.M. Cross et al, 55-107. Garden City: Doubleday, 1976.

Friedman, R.E. *The Exile and Biblical Narrative.* HSM 22. Chico, CA: Scholars, 1981.

Friedrich, J. *Phönizisch-Punische Grammatik.* AnOr 32. Rome: Pontifical Biblical Institute, 1951.

——— and Röllig, W. *Phönizisch-Punische Grammatik.* 2nd ed. AnOr 46. Pontifical Biblical Institute, 1970.

Gilula, M. "To Yahweh Shomron and to his Asherah." *Shnaton* 3 (1978/79) 129-37 (Hebrew).

Ginsberg, H.L. "Lexicographical Notes." In *Hebräische Wortforschung. Festschrift zum 80. Geburtstag von Walter Baumgartner,* 71-82. VTSup 16. Leiden: Brill, 1967.

Gordon, C. *Ugaritic Textbook.* 3 vols. AnOr 38. Rome: Pontifical Biblical Institute, 1965.

Görg, F. "Zum Namen der punischen Göttin 'Tinnit'." *UF* 11 (1979) 303-306.

Graesser, C. "Standing Stones in Ancient Palestine." *BA* 35 (1972) 34-63.

Gray, J. *The Legacy of Canaan.* VTSup 5. Leiden: Brill, 1957.

———. *The Canaanites.* London: Thames and Hudson, 1964.

———. "Social Aspects of Canaanite Religion." In *Volume du Congrès, Genève 1965,* 170-92. VTSup 15. Leiden: Brill, 1966.

———. *I & II Kings.* Old Testament Library. 2nd ed. London: SCM, 1970.

Grøndahl, F. *Die Personennamen der Texte aus Ugarit.* Studia Pohl 1. Rome: Pontifical Biblical Institute, 1967.

Gsell, S. *Histoire ancienne de l'Afrique du nord.* 8 vols. Paris: Hachette, 1920-29. Reprinted, Osnabrück: Zeller, 1972.

Güterbock, H.G. *Kumarbi, Mythen von churritischen Kronos.* New York: Europaverlag, 1946.

———. "The Song of Ullikummi: Revised Text of the Hittite Version." *JCS* 5 (1951) 135-61; 6 (1951) 8-42.

Halpern, B. "Yaua, Son of Omri, Yet Again." *BASOR* 265 (1987) 81-85.

———. " 'Brisker Pipes than Poetry': The Development of Israelite Monotheism." In *Judaic Perspectives on Ancient Israel,* 77-115. J. Neusner et al., ed. Philadelphia: Fortress, 1987.

Hamburger, H. "A Hoard of Syrian Tetradrachms and Tyrian Bronze Coins from Gush Ḥalav." *IEJ* 4 (1954) 201-26.

Hanson, P.D. "Apocalypticism." *IDBSup* 28-34.

Harden, D. *The Phoenicians.* London: Thames and Hudson, 1962.

Heider, G.C. *The Cult of Molek: A Reassessment.* Journal for the Study of the Old Testament, Supplements 43. Sheffield: Journal for the Study of the Old Testament, 1986.

Helck, W. *Die Beziehungen Ägyptens zu Vorderasien im 3. und 2. Jahrtausend v. Chr.* Ägyptologische Abhandlungen 5. Wiesbaden: Harrassowitz, 1962.

————. *Betrachtungen zur Großen Göttin und den ihr verbundenen Gottheiten*. Religion und Kultur der alten Mittelmeerwelt in Parallelforschung 2. Munich and Vienna: Oldenbourg, 1971.

———— and Otto, E. *Lexikon der Ägyptologie*. Wiesbaden: Harrassowitz, 1972.

Herdner, A. *Corpus des tablettes en cunéiformes alphabetiques découvertes à Ras-Shamra-Ugarit de 1929 à 1939*. Mission de Ras Shamra 10. Paris: Imprimerie National, 1963.

Herrmann, W. "Aštart." *Mitteilungen des Instituts für Orientforschung* 15 (1969) 6-55.

Hill, G.F. *Catalogue of the Greek Coins of Palestine*. Catalogue of the Greek Coins in the British Museum 27. London: British Museum, 1914.

Hillers, D. *Micah*. Hermeneia. Philadelphia: Fortress, 1984.

Hoffner, H.A. "The Elkunirsa Myth Reconsidered." *Revue hittite et asianique* 76 (1965) 5-16.

————. "Second Millennium Antecedents to the Hebrew 'ôb." *JBL* 86 (1967) 385-401.

————. "'ôbh." *TDOT* 1: 130-34.

Holladay, W. "On Every High Hill and Under Every Green Tree." *VT* 11 (1961) 170-76.

Horst, F. and Robinson, T. *Die Zwölfkleinenpropheten*. HAT 1/4. Tübingen: Mohr, 1964.

Hvidberg-Hansen, F.O. *La déesse Tnt, un étude sur la religion canaanéo-punique*. 2 vols. Copenhagen: Gad, 1979.

Hyatt, J.P. "Jeremiah and Deuteronomy." *JNES* 1 (1942) 156-73.

Jackson, K.P. *The Ammonite Language of the Iron Age*. HSM 27. Chico, CA: Scholars, 1983.

Jaroš, K. "Zur Inschrift Nr. 3 von Hirbet el-Qôm." *Biblische Notizen* 19 (1982) 30-41.

Kaiser, O. *Der Prophet Jesaja, Kapitel 13-39*. ATD 18. Göttingen: Vandenhoeck & Ruprecht, 1973.

Kapelrud, A.S. *Baal in the Ras Shamra Texts*. Copenhagen: Gad, 1952.

Kaufman, I.T. "The Samaria Ostraca: An Early Witness to Hebrew Writing." *BA* 45 (1982) 229-39.

Kaufman, S. "The Enigmatic Adad-Milki." *JNES* 37 (1978) 101-10.

Kutscher, E.Y. "Aramaic." *Current Trends in Linguistics* 6 (1970) 347-412.

Landsberger, B. *Sam'al.* Ankara: Druckerei der Türkischen historischen Gesellschaft, 1948.

Lapp, P. "The 1968 Excavations at Tell Ta'annek." *BASOR* 195 (1969) 2-49.

————. "A Ritual Incense Stand from Taanak." *Qadmoniot* 2 (1969) 16-17.

Lawton, R. "Israelite Personal Names on Pre-Exilic Hebrew Inscriptions." *Bib* 65 (1984) 330-46.

Leclant, J. "Astarté à cheval d'après les représentations égyptiennes." *Syria* 37 (1960) 1-67.

Lemaire, A. "Les inscriptions de Khirbet el-Qôm et l'Ashérah de Yhwh." *RB* 84 (1977) 597-608.

————. "Who or What was Yahweh's Asherah?" *Biblical Archaeology Review* 10.6 (1984) 42-51.

————. "Date et origine des inscriptions hébraïques et phéniciennes de Kuntillet 'Ajrud." *Studi epigraphici e linguistici* 1 (1984) 131-43.

Levenson, J. "Who Inserted the Book of the Torah?" *HTR* 68 (1975) 203-33.

L'Heureux, C.E. *Rank Among the Canaanite Gods.* HSM 21. Missoula, MT: Scholars, 1979.

Lidzbarski, M. *Ephemeris für semitische Epigraphik.* 3 vols. Gießen: Töpelmann, 1900-15.

Lindblom, J. *Die Jesaja-Apokalypse, Jes. 24-27.* Lund: Gleerup, 1938.

Lipiński E. "The Goddess Atirat in Ancient Arabia, in Babylonia, and in Ugarit." *Orientalia Lovaniensia Periodica* 3 (1972) 101-19.

Lohfink, N. "Auslegung deuteronomistischer Texte, IV." *Bib Leb* 5 (1964) 250-54.

————. "Deuteronomy." *IDBSup* 229-32.

————. "Dt. 26, 17-19 und die 'Bundesformel'." *ZKT* 91 (1969) 517-53.

Løkkegaard, F. "A Plea for El the Bull, and other Ugaritic Miscellanies." In *Studia Orientalia Iaonni Pedersen septuagenario dicata*, 219-35. Copenhagen: Einar Munksgaard, 1953.

————. "Baalsfald." *DTT* 19 (1956) 65-82.

————. Review of F.O. Hvidberg-Hansen, *La déesse Tnt. UF* 14 (1982) 129-40.

Long, B.O. "Divination." *IDBSup* 241-43.

Luyton, J. "Primeval and Eschatological Overtones in the Song of Moses (Dt 32, 1-43)." *Das Deuteronomium. Entstehung, Gestalt und Botschaft*, ed. N. Lohfink, 341-47. BETL 68. Leuven: Leuven University, 1985.

McCarter, P.K., Jr. "Aspects of the Religion of the Israelite Monarchy." In *Ancient Israelite Religion: Essays in Honor of Frank Moore Cross*, ed. P. Miller et al, 137-55. Philadelphia: Fortress, 1987.

McKenzie, S. *The Chronicler's Use of the Deuteronomistic History*. HSM 33. Chico, CA: Scholars, 1985.

Maier, W.A., III. *'Ašerah: Extrabiblical Evidence*. HSM 37. Atlanta: Scholars, 1986.

Margalit, B. "A Ugaritic Psalm (*RS* 24.252)." *JBL* 89 (1970) 292-304.

Mayes, A.D.H. *Deuteronomy*. New Century Bible. London: Oliphants, 1979.

Mazar, A. "The 'Bull Site'—An Iron Age I Open Cult Place." *BASOR* 247 (1982) 27-42.

Mendelsohn, I. "Divination." *IDB* 1:856-858.

Mendenhall, G. "The Worship of Baal and Asherah: A Study in the Social Bonding Function of Religious Systems." In *Biblical and Related Studies Presented to Samuel Iwry*, ed. A. Kort and S. Morschauser, 147-58. Winona Lake, IN: Eisenbrauns, 1985.

Meshel, Z. "Kuntilat 'Ajrûd—An Israelite Site from the

Monarchical period on the Sinai Border." *Qadmoniot* 9 (1976) 118-24 (Hebrew).

———. "Kuntillet 'Ajrûd—An Israelite Religious Center in the Northern Sinai." *Expedition* 20 (1978) 50-54.

———. *Kuntillet 'Ajrûd: A Religious Centre from the Time of the Judaean Monarchy.* Museum Catalogue 175. Jerusalem: Israel Museum, 1978.

———. "Did Yahweh Have a Consort?" *Biblical Archaeology Review* 5.2 (1979) 24-36.

du Mesnil du Buisson, R. *Nouvelles études sur les dieux et les mythes de Canaan.* Etudes préliminaires aux religions orientales dans l'Empire romain 33. Leiden: Brill, 1973.

Milik, J.T. Les papyrus araméens d'Hermoupolis et les cultes syro-phéniciens en Egypte perse." *Bib* 48 (1967) 546-621.

Miller, P.D. "Animal Names as Designations in Ugaritic and Hebrew." *UF* 2 (1970) 177-86.

———. "Psalms and Inscriptions." *Congress Volume, Vienna 1980*, 311-32. VTSup 32. Leiden: Brill, 1981.

Miller, W. *Isaiah 24-27 and the Origin of Apocalyptic.* HSM 11. Missoula, MT: Scholars, 1976.

Mittmann, S. "Die Grabinschrift des Sängers Uriahu." *ZDPV* 97 (1981) 139-52.

de Moor, J.C. "*'ăshērāh.*" *TDOT* 1: 438-44.

Moran, W.L. "The Ancient Near Eastern Background of the Love of God in Deuteronomy." *CBQ* 25 (1963) 77-87.

Mosca, P. "Child Sacrifice in Canaanite and Israelite Religion." Ph.D. dissertation, Harvard University, 1975.

Moscati, S. *The World of the Phoenicians.* New York: Praeger, 1968.

———. "L'origine de 'segno di Tanit'." *Accademia nazionale dei Lincei, Rendiconti.* 8/27.

Mowinckel, S. *Zur Komposition des Buches Jeremia.* Oslo: Dybwad, 1914.

Mullen, T. *The Divine Council in Canaanite and Early Hebrew Literature.* HSM 24. Chico, CA: Scholars, 1980.

Na'aman, N. "Sennacherib's 'Letter to God' on his Campaign to Judah." *BASOR* 214 (1974) 25-39.

Naveh, J. "Graffiti and Dedications." *BASOR* 235 (1979) 27-30.

Noth, M. *Exodus.* Old Testament Library. Philadelphia: Westminster, 1962.

Nougayrol, J. et al. eds. *Ugaritica V.* Mission de Ras Shamra 16. Paris: Imprimerie Nationale, 1968.

Nowack, W. *Die kleinen Propheten.* Göttingen Handkommentar zum Alten Testament 3/4. Göttingen: Vandenhoeck & Ruprecht, 1922.

Oden, R. "The Persistence of Canaanite Religion." *BA* 39 (1976) 31-36.

———. *"Ba'al Šamēm and 'Ēl."* *CBQ* 39 (1977) 457-73.

———. *Studies in Lucian's De Syria Dea.* HSM 15. Missoula, MT: Scholars, 1977.

Oldenburg, U. *The Conflict Between El and Ba'al in Canaanite Religion.* Leiden: Brill, 1969.

del Olmo Lete, G. *Mitos y Leyendas de Canaan. Segun la Tradicion de Ugarit.* Institucion San Jeronimo Fuentes de la Ciencia Biblica 1. Madrid: Ediciones Cristiandad, 1981.

Olyan, S.M. *"Hăšālôm*: Some Literary Considerations of 2 Kings 9." *CBQ* 46 (1984) 652-68.

———. "The Cultic Confessions of Jer 2, 27a." *ZAW* 99 (1987) 254-59.

———. "Some Observations Concerning the Identity of the Queen of Heaven." *UF* 19 (1988) forthcoming.

——— and Smith, M.S. Review of G. Heider, *The Cult of Molek. RB* 94 (1987) 273-75.

Otten, H. "Ein kanaanäischer Mythus aus Boğazköy." *Mitteilungen des Instituts für Orientforschung* 1 (1953) 125-50.

———. "Kanaanäische Mythen aus Hattusa-Boğazköy." MDOG 85 (1953) 27-38.

Otzen, B. "Traditions and Structures of Isaiah xxiv-xxvii." *VT* 24 (1974) 196-211.

Le Palais royal d'Ugarit. Paris: Imprimerie Nationale, 1957-.

Pardee, D. "The Preposition in Ugaritic." *UF* 7 (1975) 329-78; 8 (1976) 215-322.

―――. "Letters from Tel Arad." *UF* 10 (1978) 289-336.

―――. Review of C.E. L'Heureux, *Rank Among the Canaanite Gods*. *AfO* 28 (1981/82) 265-67.

―――. "An Evaluation of the Proper Names from Ebla from a West Semitic Perspective: Pantheon Distribution According to Genre." Forthcoming, in the proceedings of the conference "The Onomasticon of Ebla: Semitic Name-Giving and Eblaic Prosopography," Rome, 15-17 Luglio, 1985.

Patai, R. "The Goddess Asherah." *JNES* 24 (1965) 37-52.

Peckham, J.B. *The Development of the Late Phoenician Scripts*. Harvard Semitic Studies 20. Cambridge: Harvard University, 1968.

Petrie, W.F. *Ancient Gaza V*. London: British School of Egyptian Archaeology, 1952.

Pohl, A. "Zu 4 Könige 17,31." *Bib* 22 (1941) 35-37.

Pope, M.H. *El in the Ugaritic Texts*. Leiden: Brill, 1955.

―――. "Ups and Downs in El's Amours." *UF* 11 (1979) 701-708.

―――― and Röllig, W. "Syrien. Die Mythologie der Ugariter und Phönizier." *Wörterbuch der Mythologie*, ed. H.W. Haussig. 2 vols. Stuttgart: Klett, 1965. 1:217-312.

―――. "Notes on the Rephaim Texts." In *Essays on the Ancient Near East in Memory of Jacob Joel Finkelstein*, ed. M. de Jong Ellis, 163-82. Hamden, CT: Archon, 1977.

―――. "The Cult of the Dead at Ugarit." In *Ugarit in Retrospect: Fifty Years of Ugarit and Ugaritic*, ed. G.W. Young, 159-79. Winona Lake, IN: Eisenbrauns, 1981.

―――. Review of C.E. L'Heureux, *Rank Among the Canaanite Gods*. *BASOR* 251 (1983) 67-69.

Porten, B. *Archives from Elephantine*. Berkeley and Los Angeles: University of California, 1968.

Pratt, R. "Controversy in Exile." Seminar paper, Harvard University, 1984.

Pritchard, J.B., ed. *The Ancient Near East in Pictures Relating to the Old Testament.* Princeton: Princeton University, 1954.

―――. *Ancient Near Eastern Texts Relating to the Old Testament.* 3rd ed. Princeton: Princeton University, 1969.

―――. *Recovering Sarepta, A Phoenician City.* Princeton: Princeton University, 1978.

―――. "The Tanit Inscription from Sarepta." In *Phönizier im Westen*, ed. H.G. Niemeyer, 83-92. Madrider Beiträge 8. Mainz: Zabern, 1982.

von Rad, G. *Deuteronomy.* Old Testament Library. Philadelphia: Westminster, 1966.

Rainey, A.F. "Verbal Usages in the Taanach Texts." *Israel Oriental Studies* 7 (1977) 33-64.

Ranke, H. *Ägyptischen Personennamen.* Glückstadt: J.J. Augsustin, 1977.

Reed, W.L. *The Asherah in the Old Testament.* Fort Worth: Texas Christian University, 1949.

―――. "Asherah." *IDB* 1:250-52.

Ringgren, H. *Israelite Religion.* Philadelphia: Fortress, 1966.

Robertson, D.A. *Linguistic Evidence in Dating Early Hebrew Poetry.* SBLDS 3. Missoula, MT: Society of Biblical Literature, 1972.

Rofé, A. "The Covenant in the Land of Moab (Dt 28,69-30,20): Historico-literary, Comparative and Formcritical Considerations." In *Das Deuteronomium*, ed. N. Lohfink, 310-20.

Rosenbaum, J. "Hezekiah's Reform and the Deuteronomistic Tradition." *HTR* 72 (1979) 23-43.

Rudolph, W. *Hosea.* KAT 13/1. Gütersloh: Mohn, 1966.

Schmidt, W. *Königtum Gottes in Ugarit und Israel.* BZAW 80. Berlin: De Gruyter, 1961.

Silverman, M.H. *Religious Values in the Jewish Proper Names at Elephantine.* AOAT 217. Neukirchen-Vluyn: Neukirchener/Kevelaer: Butzon & Bercker, 1985.

Smith, M.S. "Divine Travel as a Token of Divine Rank." *UF* 16 (1984) 359.

———. "Kothar-wa-Ḥasis, the Ugaritic Craftsman God." Ph.D. dissertation, Yale University, 1985.

von Soden, W. *Akkadisches Handwörterbuch.* 3 vols. Wiesbaden: Harrassowitz, 1965-81.

Sola Solé, J.M. "Inscripciones Fenicias de la Península Ibérica." *Sefarad* 15 (1955) 41-53.

Stadelmann, R. *Syrisch-Palästinensische Gottheiten in Ägypten.* Probleme der Ägypologie 5. Leiden: Brill, 1967.

Stager, L. and Wolff, S. "Child Sacrifice at Carthage—Religious Rite or Population Control?" *Biblical Archaeology Review* 10.1 (1984) 31-51.

Stolz, F. "Monotheismus in Israel." In *Monotheismus im alten Israel und seiner Umwelt,* ed. O. Keel, 143-89. Biblische Beiträge 14. Fribourg: Schweizerisches Katholisches Bibelwerk, 1980.

Stockton, E. "Stones at Worship." *AJBA* 1 (1970) 58-81.

Tigay, J. *You Shall Have No Other Gods. Israelite Religion in the Light of Hebrew Inscriptions.* Harvard Semitic Studies 31. Atlanta: Scholars, 1986.

Timm, S. *Die Dynastie Omri.* FRLANT 124. Göttingen: Vandenhoeck & Ruprecht, 1982.

de Vaux, R. Review of A. Alt, "Die Stadtstaat Samaria." *RB* 63 (1956) 100-106.

———. *Ancient Israel.* New York: McGraw-Hill, 1961.

———. *Studies in Old Testament Sacrifice.* Cardiff: University of Wales, 1964.

———. "Téman, ville ou région d'Edom?" *RB* 76 (1969) 379-85.

Wallace, H. *The Eden Narrative.* HSM 32., Atlanta: Scholars, 1985.

Weinfeld, M. *Deuteronomy and the Deuteronomic School.* Oxford: Clarendon, 1972.

———. "The Worship of Moloch and the Queen of Heaven." *UF* 4 (1972) 133-54.

———. "Kuntillet 'Ajrud Inscriptions and their Significance." *Studi epigraphici e linguistici* 1 (1984) 121-30.

————. "The Emergence of the Deuteronomic Movement: The Historical Antecedents." In *Das Deuteronomium*, ed. N. Lohfink, 76-98.

Weippert, H. *Die Prosareden des Jeremiabuches*. Berlin: De Gruyter, 1973.

Weiser, A. *Die Propheten Hosea, Joel, Amos, Obadja, Jona, Micha*. ATD 24. Göttingen: Vandenhoeck & Ruprecht, 1974.

Wellhausen, J. *Die kleinen Propheten*. 3rd ed. Berlin: Reimer, 1898.

————. *Prolegomena to the History of Ancient Israel*. Reprinted, Gloucester, MA: P. Smith, 1973.

Wilderberger, H. *Jesaja 13-27*. BKAT 10/7-12. Neukirchen-Vluyn: Neukirchener, 1974-78.

Willis, J.T. "The Authenticity and Meaning of Micah 5:9-14." *ZAW* 81 (1969) 353-68.

Wolff, H.W. *Hosea*. Hermeneia. Philadelphia: Fortress, 1974.

————. *Dodekapropheton Micha*. BKAT 14/12-14. Neukirchen-Vluyn: Neukirchener, 1980-82.

Wright, G.E. "The Lawsuit of God: A Form-Critical Study of Deuteronomy 32." In *Israel's Prophetic Heritage*, ed. B. Anderson and W. Harrelson, 26-67. New York: Harper, 1962.

Yadin, Y. et al. *Hazor II: An Account of the Second Season of Excavations, 1956*. Jerusalem: Hebrew University, 1960.

————. "Symbols of Deities at Zinjirli, Carthage and Hazor." In *Near Eastern Archaeology in the Twentieth Century. Essays in Honor of Nelson Glueck*, ed. J. Sanders, 199-231. Garden City: Doubleday, 1970.

Zevit, Z. "The Khirbet el-Qôm Inscription Mentioning a Goddess." *BASOR* 255 (1984) 39-47.

Index of Passages

Index of Authors

Index of Subjects